SUGAR IN A SHOE BOX

Joyce McFarland

AROUND H.I.M. PUBLISHING

Around His Image Marketing And Publishing

Copyright © March 2000, Joyce McFarland

Literary Editor, Sheila M. Hightower

Published by Around H.I.M. Publishing
For publishing information, address:

Around His Image Marketing and Publishing
PO Box 1373
Wake Forest, NC 27588
info@aroundHim.com
(919) 275-0446

ALL RIGHTS RESERVED
No part of this publication may be reproduced in
whole or in part, or transmitted in any form or by any
means electronic, mechanical, photocopying, or
otherwise, without written permission of the
Publisher.

ISBN-13: 978-0615489537
ISBN-10: 0615489532

DEDICATION

This book is dedicated to my birth Mother, Luretha, now deceased, who in addition to the Good Lord, gave me life. To Grandma who raised me as her very own child. To Mama Mary Florence, the only Mama I've ever known and the only Mama I was meant to know, whose faith and love has molded me and made me who I am today. To my Daddy Jimmy, who is doing what he loves to do most -- talking to God, except now, he's doing it face to face.

Sugar in a Shoebox is also dedicated to my brothers and sisters who lived the stories with me and helped create the memories. To Aunt Nee, whose glorious new legs can't stop dancing in heaven. To Cousin Les, whose humor still makes me laugh out loud. To Brown who calmed my fears after I swallowed a penny. To all my family who nurtured me and loved me, not because they had to but because they wanted to, and to Grandma Sudie, who loved me enough to hurt my pride and sometimes my backside; she also helped me see that every goodbye ain't gone. I love you, I appreciate you and I thank you all!

FOREWORD

I believe you are going to enjoy this book. Knowing Joyce McFarland for over 20+ years now, I can see why she has this magnetism with people. The stories that she writes about are humorous and heartfelt; her life pilgrimage has shaped her into a very creative writer. In this book, "Sugar in a Shoebox" are the stories of a little girl who saw the world around her in a very optimistic way. I enjoyed her creative writing skills; in fact, she will make you see life as a grand adventure. In my profession as a Pastor, I see people every day who are seeking joy and in need of hope. What a refreshing book to send you back to a simpler time. What an impact Joyce has had in my ministry; the way she connects our young with our elderly in stories and plays, is indeed a blessing from the Lord. As you read this book, you will find yourself "remembering" your own stories. I expected something honest, humorous, inspirational and challenging; it was indeed, all that and more.

Dr. Jeffrey Chapman, Sr.
Founder and Senior Pastor
Raleigh North Christian Center
Owner and founder of Technology Resolution Inc.

Table of Contents

CHAPTER 1

<u>In the Place of Soles</u>

What is the measure of a man or woman? In my case, it was 32 ounces, or four cups, or two pounds. That's what I weighed when I came into the world on a cold November night, fifty some odd years ago. Born to a very sick and frightened eighteen year old girl whose only crime was being like God made her: artistically beautiful and rich in the glorious hue of the fruit of the pecan tree.

The rural south in the fifties was still steeped in the old thoughts and opinions of eras long passed: Thoughts that one man was ordained by The Maker to be inferior to another. A place where unfounded feelings ran deep and strong. The very south itself was a school of thought that passionately believed that the lives of some were priceless, while the lives of others were without worth.

Maybe I couldn't wait to get out and change the world, or perhaps it was to fulfill some specific purpose, but whatever the reason, my arrival was about eight weeks ahead of schedule.

Have you ever looked at a two-pound bag of sugar? It might be enough to sweeten a couple pitchers of tea and a glass or two of lemonade – provided you are not a sugar holic. But, I ask you, what does one do with a two pound baby? One that could fit in the palm of your hand, one with no hair, no fingernails or toenails, no palate in the roof of her mouth; one whose eye sockets were half way down her sunken cheeks; a little girl who only had the whites of her eyes, and skin so thin you could see through it. The doctor sure didn't know or didn't care, for you see, his very words to my Mama were, "Take this thing home and let it die." But, the devil is a liar! My God, I would have you to know, I had a Grandmama who refused to accept this pronouncement from anyone! The lioness rose up within her and her faith became a voice to be reckoned with as she proclaimed; "Not so, for The Lord and me will bring her through." I now know, with every fiber of my being to this day, this very day -- the minute she spoke those words -- that's when the miracle began to happen in my life.

So my Grandmama took her 'po' little sick daughter (my birth mother), with her 'po' little puny grandbaby back to her house, so that she and the good Lord could begin the work they had to do to make mere man (the doctor) out of a lie.

My Grandmama was a woman filled with wisdom and trust in the Lord. She took me, this two pound lump of quivering flesh and put me in the only thing that would accommodate my size and Grandmama's purpose --a shoe box. Grandma lined that shoebox with the softest materials she could find. Next she filled a medium-sized mason jar filled with warm water and wrapped it in cloths so it would not burn the delicate skin of this teeny baby. Into this home-made incubator I went, the barely viable form of a tiny human, clinging to life --struggling to live. Every inch of that shoe box, from top to bottom, from side to side, inside and out, was filled to overflowing with an everlasting love, fortified and saturated with prayer.

Grandmama would empty and refill the mason jar every hour, replacing the cooled water with warm water. The only fireplace in the house, other than the one in the kitchen, was in the sitting room. The shoebox and its contents were pushed close to the wall next to that fireplace, so as to keep the little life as warm as possible. Every hour, Grandmama would feed me from an eye dropper filled with formula made with evaporated milk. All through the days and all through the nights, Grandmama and Grandma Sudie nursed and prayed, sang and prayed and prayed and prayed, so that a death sentence pronounced at birth would not come to pass.

I've been told by all my family who were big enough to remember that my Mama (my birth mother) loved me so very much. She was so afraid she would hurt me, because I was so tiny, that she would carry me around on a pillow rather than in her arms. They told me how she would gently stroke my skin as she would sing to me and talked to me all the time.

My Mama was very sick, but no one knew just how sick she was. The trauma of childbirth, along with an undiagnosed ailment that she had been plagued with for some time, were just too much for her frail body to endure. She never recuperated, and before daybreak one morning, three months after bringing me into this world, she slipped peacefully away into the waiting arms of Jesus, leaving her precious gift, me, to her Mama (Mary Florence) and family.

From that point on, Grandmama Mary Florence became Mama; Granddaddy Carcy became Daddy; all their young'uns became my sisters and brothers; and nobody from that day to this one has ever seen it any other way.

It took many months of tender loving care, prayer and determination to bring these 32 ounces of unlovely, (some thought incurable), helpless mass of flesh to a healthy, happy, round faced, bright eyed, curly head bouncing baby girl. But what a reward for Mama's efforts when she took me back to that doctor, just to give him a look and see. This is how it went: About ten months later she carried me back to the place where I was born and asked to see that same doctor who assisted with my delivery –to bring me into the world. When she stood face to face with him she asked him this question; "Doctor, do you know who this baby is?" His brisk and curt reply was simply, "No." Then she proudly proceeded to hold up for his inspection the prettiest, chubbiest, happiest little cooing baby he would ever see. With these words she pierced the innermost chamber of his heart; "This is that *"thing"* that you told me to take home and let die." My Mama said she could see the years of his haughtiness and his great swelling arrogance crumble as he stood there staring in the shining eyes of this precious child who unwittingly held out her hands to him as the tears of shame and humility cascaded down his cheeks.

GOD HAS A WAY! What He means to be --will be. What He purposes to be --will come to pass. What He starts rest assured --He will finish. If you don't believe it just ask the "Little Shoebox Girl."

CHAPTER 2

Grandma, please don't put that snuff on my face!

But she would anyway. Just let a bee or a wasp or a mean ole yellow jacket pop that sting up side my head or any other body parts of mine, and Grandma would appear from nowhere. She'd thrust her pointing finger inside her lip and pull it out covered in brown, icky wet snuff that had been in her mouth since 4:30a.m. that morning when she helped cook breakfast for Daddy, all us "chiren" and sundry kinfolk. I knew she was going to plaster that stung place with enough snuff to take the poison out of six bee stings.

Do you think she cared that I almost lost my insides when I saw that thick glob of wet gook heading straight for me? NOPE, not one little bit. All she cared about was that it would make her sweet little "Goosey" not hurt anymore. And Grandma was right! As soon as she spread that snuff on my sting it would stop hurting and the swelling would go down immediately. I tell you, nothing on the market today works as quick and inexpensive as Grandma Sudie's snuff. Of course I believe what worked more than the healing properties of the snuff was the love with which it was applied.

My Grandma Sudie didn't have a lot of "egecation," but she did have a lot of what old folks called "mother wit." You see, that's when the old folks know what you're attempting to do before you do it. I recall the time when I was about eight years old. I loved to sing and put on a show. Young'uns still love to do that today. You see, I kind of pictured myself as the colored version of Annette Funicello of the Mickey Mouse Club or a younger, skinny replica of the beautiful and mighty Mahalia Jackson.

Anyhow, everybody was in the fields working that day and me and Grandma Sudie was home alone. Grandma was outside washing collard greens or something --you know, doing what grandmas do. My Daddy had one of them long drop cords with the light thing attached to the end. He used it to hang in the little wooden box to keep the new little biddies (baby pigs) warm and when he was working on something under the hood of our car. I was in the house thinking up something to do. Walla! I know what -- I'll get me a microphone and perform. So I get Daddy's light thing (there was no bulb in it), plug it in and start belting out, "Nobody Knows The Trouble I See".

Suddenly, Grandma Sudie busts through the door, yanks the plug out of the outlet, grabs me by both shoulders and yells in my face, "young'un is you crazy!" I tell you, I was so shocked and scared at the wild-eyed look on her face that I couldn't say a word.

"Lord have mercy", she said, "somethin' told me I better git in this house and see what you was up to. I'm so glad I listened." Then her voice softened and

14

she hugged me and said, "Baby that there cord is dangerous with no light bulb in it. You could have stuck your finger in it or even your tongue and it could have killed you. God knows they'da had to carry your Grandma out too. Now you git outta here and go play."

Mother wit has saved a lot of foolish young'uns!

BEE STING CURE

1. A glob of wet Sweet Railroad Mills Snuff from at least a six hour-old "cud." (Cud - snuff that has been in the lip since who knows when.)

2. One pointing finger calloused by years of serving others.

3. Enough spit to make it stick.

4. Most of all, applied with love in abundance.

5. It's great to have fantasies and dreams; just don't destroy yourself before you can live them out.

6. Young'uns are still the same – even today; they cannot see the dangers in life.

CHAPTER 3

Grandma, why can't I be in there with y'all?

One thing old folks did not put up with was young'uns listening to grown folks' conversations. No siree! That would get you a whipping just about quicker than anything else you could do.

Grandma use to say, "chiren ain't got no business in grown folks' business. It'll make 'em grown before they time." You know what - now I know my Grandma was right. Anyway, I remember one time after church one Sunday, my Grandma Sudie, my Aunt Annie, (Grandma's daughter), Uncle Ervin,(Aunt Annie's husband) and I went to visit this real, real old couple that my Grandma knew. It was in the Fall season --the time of the year when it gets dark earlier. This old man and his wife lived so far back in the woods that even the night owls were afraid to go back in there. Of course, it goes without saying they had no electricity and no running water inside their house. They had no grandchildren, no dog nor cat, and mercy me, no radio or TV so, guess what? I sat there in this big old dark, damp feeling, musky smelling, shadowy room on a huge scratchy couch by myself, listening with held breath to every creak and groan of that old house. The adults had all gone to a room in the back of the house; Uncle Ervin and the old man were in the kitchen drinking coffee and the women folk were in the bedroom looking at some dress material the old woman had bought.

I sat there stiff as a board with eyes as big as saucers while the shadows in the room played tricks on me. Was that a coat hanging over the back of a chair or was that a man with no head? Did I just see what I thought I saw? Was that a little mouse that just ran across the floor or a big ole wharf rat with huge jagged teeth? Oh my, what is that scratching at the door? Why did it get so cold in here all of a sudden? Hey what was it that just rubbed across the back of my neck? Where is that smell like rotten eggs coming from? I thought I was in this dark room by myself, so who or what is doing all that heavy breathing?

The kerosene lamp is flickering and the flame is going out. That's my only protection against what may lurk in the dark. "Oh Lord Mama, I'm scared." Is that a pair of eyes peering in the window? What's that big black fuzzy thing crawling up the wall over there? Help me somebody! Something's creeping up my leg! The darkness, the smell, the creaking and groaning sounds and a huge black cat that jumped on the back of the couch from out of nowhere finally took their toll on me, so I ran from the room to where the women were and sat down --heart just a pounding! I never uttered a word, mind you; I just sat down. But my mere presence was enough. My stern but sweet Aunt Annie, who by the way, had no young'uns of her own, gently took me by the hand and looked squarely into

18

my eyes and said, "Hain't I told you not to be trying to hear what grown folks be talkin 'bout?" All I could whimper was, "Yes Mam." "Come on here then," she said, "I'll learn you to listen when I tell you somethin'." We fumbled our way through the dark 'til we got outside. She aptly reached up in a China Ball Tree, broke off a switch, and went to town on my fanny. I tell you the truth, I remember nothing after that but waking up in the car in our front yard an hour or so later.

Ever since then, grown folks' conversations don't interest me --no siree, not one bit.

RAISING RESPECTFUL CHILDREN

1. Don't talk about everything and everybody in front of them.

2. Do not let them hear you talking "dirty", or they will too.

3. REMEMBER, they are children, not adults and should not be burdened with adult problems.

4. It's from your mouth to their ears.

5. Fear will chase you from one danger right into another one.

6. There are some kinds of fear that's good – the fears that numb you so you can't feel pain.

CHAPTER 4

<u>A dog named Bee Bop</u>

Out in the country, everybody had at least one dog. Most of them were "sooners", (sooner be this kind, or sooner be that kind). So you can be sure that there was a whole lot of barking going on from house to house.

We had a beautiful dog that was part German Shepherd and part collie. My sister's boyfriend, Brown, who later became my brother-in-law, got the dog in Dunn from a man named Mr. John McQueen. Mr. John was a strong believer in roots, and I don't mean herbs. Anyway, we named our little puppy Bee Bop. He slept in a box of straw on our back porch until he got big enough to sleep under the pump shelter. Mama would not stand for any dogs or cats to be in the house and she would not let us eat at anyone's house who did.

I loved that little dog so much. I would put him in a cardboard box and carry him around all day. (Daddy would not let us hold him a lot because he said that would make him wormy.) He was my baby doll. All of us children fed him and took real good care of him and at night when he would whine, we would go out and sit on the porch with him. He grew into a very big dog with a ferocious growl and a deep bass bark.

My Daddy raised pigs and sometimes they would get out of the pen through a hole in the fence.

Bee Bop would chase them pigs until he ran every single one of them back through the hole into the pen again, but he never would bite them or hurt them.

That dog loved to chase cars more than he loved to eat when he was hungry. When he'd hear a car coming down the road, he would run out to the side of the ditch bank and stand. As soon as the car got in front of our house, he would take off running alongside of it at break neck speed. He would always run along the shoulder of the road but he never would run on the road. He would chase the car for about two tenths of a mile, then he'd turn around and come back home.

Anyone could come onto our porch without Bee Bop raising a ruckus --as long as some of us were outside with him. But, if we were inside, the person could only come as far as the yard.

There was a wonderful family that lived down the road a piece from us. The daddy would get drunk every weekend. He always came to visit us because he loved my Daddy and my Mama. One night after we had gone to bed, we heard Bee Bop just a barking and growling at something. There was a lot of commotion on the front porch and someone was hollering and making a real loud racket. All of us jumped up and ran to the porch just in time to see our drunken neighbor high tailing it across the front yard with all the backside of his pants torn out and dangling. Bee Bop was in hot pursuit! We were all laughing so hard; my Daddy could hardly regain his composure enough to calm Bee Bop down. That po drunken man never stopped running until he reached home. I'm sure his wife was all too grateful 'cause he had run all the alcohol out of his system.

Mama and Grandma didn't get on too well with Bee Bop though, 'cause he would not let them whip us young'uns when he was around. If they tried to whip us outside, Bee Bop would jump all over them, snarling and barking like he was going to eat them up. If they took us inside to whip us, he would come to the window or on the porch and try and get in the house when he would hear us crying. Anytime one of us was going to get a switching, someone would have to put Bee Bop in the barn and shut the door.

After he was let out of the barn, he would go to where the whipped young'un was and lie down right beside 'em.

Bee Bop was my "best" friend in the whole wide world.

HOW TO SOBER A DRUNK

1. A dark night

2. A big ferocious dog

3. A long way home.

4. The wind in their breeches.

CHAPTER 5

Grandma hide me please! It's Red Eyes and Bloody Bones!!!

When I was little there were all kinds of strange folks that lived out in the country, but they were for the most part harmless.

Old folks use to tell young'uns that the boogie man would get them if they were bad, and that seemed to be enough to keep the children pretty well behaved. My folks didn't use that boogie man line -- no siree; they had a far better one: a living, breathing, honest to goodness skeleton looking acquaintance by the name of Mr. June Oaks, better known to us young'uns as "Red Eyes and Bloody Bones".

He was about 6'5" and weighed about 100 pounds. At least that's what he looked like to a first grader. His cheeks were all sunk in and his hair was cut real close to his head. He had very big eyes that always looked red and watery. He walked stooped over but took long slow strides. He carried an old greasy, dirty burlap sack slung over his back all the time, and he walked everywhere he went. Grandma said the bones of mean "chiren" were in that bag.

Whatever we young'uns were doing, no matter whether we were in the house or in the yard when we spotted him coming, we would run and get as close up beside Grandma as we could. Old Red Eyes and Bloody Bones would always end up in our kitchen 'cause he loved coffee, and Mama would always fix him something to eat.

We would watch him from behind Grandma's skirt tails. Grandma would say, "It's all right. He's not gonna bother y'all today 'cause y'all been good 'chiren', and it looks like he's got enough bones in that bag to last him a while." We never took our eyes off of him, not for one minute, the whole time he was there. When he was at our house, we were so quiet that no one could tell that young'uns even lived there unless they saw us. He never talked much, just sat there and ate, and drank lots of Louisiana coffee with chicory, all the while keeping that old sack right next to him. After the meal he'd reach into the sack and pull out what we young'uns just knew was a splinter from some "po" child's bone and pick his teeth, all the while leering at us. Then after what seemed like an eternity, he'd reach out with that long bony hand and take the food Mama had wrapped up for him, pick up his sack and head on back down the road.

He didn't come often or stay very long, but his memory would linger long enough to squash any rebellious, disobedient behavior in us young'uns for at least a week.

BOOGIE MAN REFLECTIONS

1. Old men don't scare children anymore; now children scare old men.

2. Nothing in real life can be as scary as what's on Saturday morning cartoons and television prime time.

3. There is no such-a-thing as a boogie man. Boogie nights, yes! Boogie fever, yes! Boogie woogie, yes!, but no boogie man.

4. Have you all ever noticed, they never say boogie woman?

CHAPTER 6

Look out Roadrunner, here comes Goosey!!

When we moved from the country to town, I could out run every boy on my street. We would have races coming home from school and I was always declared the fastest thing on legs. Living in the country with all the wide spaces in which to run and all the things that caused me to run were the principal reasons I could run so fast.

You see, when you are the baby girl and you have brothers who like to play tricks on you, you develop a lot of survival skills that you might otherwise never learn. We lived beside the highway out in Harnett County during the fifties. The road was a decent tar and asphalt one, but it had some mighty awesome curves in some places. One of those curves was about two tenths of a mile from our house. It was such a bad curve that cars and motorcycles were always turning over there, seriously hurting and sometimes killing the drivers and their passengers. So, we young'uns named it Dead Man's Curve. The only store for miles around was about one half mile beyond this curve. There was no other way around it; you had to walk the curve to get to the store.

It never ever failed that my Mama would always need something from that store late in the evening, right before supper time. She would send one or both of my older brothers, Bob and Mickey, so me and my knee baby sister Sudie Mae would always beg to go along (bad idea, tho). Grandma would give us all a nickel or a dime a piece to buy us some goodies. Back then you could get a lot of stuff for a few cents. A big Baby Ruth Candy Bar only cost five cents and a Sugar Daddy was a nickel too. You could get two big Johnnie Cake Cookies for one cent and hard sucking candies were two for a penny.

We'd meander around and play along the road, so by the time we'd start back home from the store, it would be just about dusk dark. Just as sure as grits is grocery, my brothers would get right to that Dead Man's Curve and start pointing and yelling, "Look over yonder in the field. It's a man with no head and he's gonna git us." Then the two of them would start running. Me and Sudie Mae would be running and screaming, scared out of our minds.

Bob and Mickey wouldn't stop running to see about us either. We never wore shoes in the Summer and the sound of our bare feet hitting the pavement was like people clapping their hands in church after a rousing song by the choir. I tell you, these two little girls were scared out of our wits and we would run so fast, that when we'd get to our house, we would be so out of breath that we couldn't even talk. Bob and Mickey and the rest of the family would all be standing on the front porch laughing their heads off. I think that was always a source of great entertainment for everybody except me and Sudie Mae. One time we were running so fast, that we ran right passed our house and our brothers had to catch up with us to bring us back. Daddy and Mama would give them boys a good scolding whenever they could stop laughing long enough themselves, but it didn't matter, 'cause they played the same kind of trick on us the very next time we went to the store with them. Now that I look back on it, my sister and I never missed a chance to go to the store, even though we knew what was going to happen. After all, being scared out your skull is a small sacrifice to make for a bag full of two for a penny candy.

My Daddy would sometimes be way back down behind our house plowing fields next to the woods, and Mama would send me with a quart mason jar of ice water or lemonade for him. I didn't want the ice to melt in the jar so I would run with it as fast as I could. I liked taking Daddy that cold drink, `cause he would stop the mule or the tractor and sit down right on the ground; just me and him, drinking whatever was in the jar. Then he'd ask about what Mama was cooking and sometimes he would let me ride on the tractor with him for a row or two. Then I'd take the empty jar and run back home as fast as I could so I could get a piece of candy or chewing gum that Grandma would give me for carrying the water to Daddy. When I look back on them days, I believe that I spent most of `em running "to" or running "from" something or somebody. Hey, I was running before running was "cool".

WHEN TO RUN FOR YOUR LIFE

1. When being chased by a headless person.

2. When the bravest people are running faster than you.

3. When the unknown is at your heels and home is in sight.

4. When you are taking something to someone you dearly love 'cause they are in need.

5. When there is a sweet reward waiting for you at the end.

CHAPTER 7

Grandma, why do I have to go and get my own switch?

According to my Grandma Sudie I could be so mean when I was a little girl. My Grandma said my moods worked with the moon. I got more whippings on the full moon than at any other time. Course to hear Grandma tell it, I was like a young'un possessed by an imp (a devilish spirit that just couldn't keep out of trouble).

You know, she might have been on to something 'cause I always had more than my share of energy and I would always think of wild things to do. I never could sleep straight through the night either. This was a source of pure aggravation for my sisters and Grandma. I slept in the same bed with two of my sisters, Shirley and Sudie Mae, until I tossed and turned so much that they would put me out and made me sleep with Grandma. Grandma was so sweet about letting me come in her bed, but she smelled like lye soap and liniment.

Lye soap you say? Yes! She and Mama would make it out of grease, lye and water in a big black wash pot in the back yard. They would put skimping of used Camay Soap in it to make it smell good, especially if it was to be used for washing our body.

They would let me stir the pot with a huge wooden paddle while they put wood on the fire underneath it. We washed our bodies with the Soap and it made our skin feel so smooth and soft. We also used it to wash our clothes and our dishes. Everything came so clean.

Well, I would do little no no's, like not come when I was called, or talk back (sass), or stick my fingers in my ears and sing to the top of my voice when I was being reprimanded by a grown up. Sure 'nuff, Grandma didn't play that. She'd say, "Gal, go get me a switch right now." So off I would go, as slow as I could walk (and get away with it) down to the edge of the corn patch. I would get the skinniest, scrawniest little switch I could find from the tall growing weeds. Then I'd sash shay back to Grandma just as pleased with myself as I could be. Grandma would take that little switch and say, "Gal, you call this a switch? Go back down there and get me two more, and they better not look like this "un" either!" The torture of going back down there to get two more switches to wail my backside was punishment enough, so I thought. This time I would spend about five minutes trying to pick out two that were not too big or too small. Finally, after choosing what I thought would be sufficient, I'd slow poke it on back to where Grandma was waiting. To my surprise, she would think these were too little too. But instead of sending me back again, she would skillfully plait the three together to make one long, strong braided switch.

Then she'd commence to burning my backside –good fashion.

Usually, after one of Grandma's whippings, I would find it soothing to curl up on Mama's bed and go to sleep. When I woke up, there would be Grandma loving on me and saying sweet things to me and making my little heart swell with love for her. Daddy and Mama never tried to keep me from getting a whipping. They knew that Grandma did it because she loved me and wanted me to be the kind of person that others would love too.

It never crossed my mind to be upset or mad after a whipping. Somehow, even as a young'un, I knew that my Grandma and my parents loved me so much and that giving me a whipping, disciplining me, was another way of showing their love for me.

I now know for me, those whippings (done in love), have given me the character and behavior that has sustained me throughout my life.

SWITCHING vs. TIMEOUT vs. NO ACTION

1. Timeout is for the grownups so they can get the young'un out of their face for a while and not deal with the problem.

2. Doing or saying nothing lets the young'un know that the grownups aren't concerned enough to respond, so the young'un thinks that his/her bad behavior is okay.

3. If you plant corn, the weeds will come up too.

4. Maybe all parents ought to move to the country where the switches are more plentiful.

CHAPTER 8

How many people does it really take to make a home?

My family was a fairly large family living under one roof. There was Daddy, Mama, Grandpa Tom, Grandma Sudie, three brothers; Jay Bird, ('cause he could sing so pretty), Mickey and Bob; three sisters, Lois, Shirley and Sudie Mae; Aunt Nee (Daddy's sister), and me. There was always an extra relative or two who would come and stay with us for a good amount of time. One of our favorite relatives was Mama's second cousin, Lester, who was blind. We called him Cousin Les. He was so loved by the family, that the children of later years called him "Uncle" Cousin Les.

He was an extraordinary man who could do so many things and do them very well. He said that he could see images when he was younger, but as he got older, his sight worsened to the point where he was classified legally blind. He never attended school or had any formal training on how to manage without his sight, but he chopped wood, built fires in the stove, washed dishes, helped in the kitchen, made beds, swept floors, washed and ironed his own clothes, polished shoes and even combed and braided my hair. He would baby sit for my nieces and nephews in later years and he even did a little cooking. He could make out what denomination paper money was just by the feel of it and he could count as well as anybody.

He was a laugh a minute. He kept some hilarious conversations going all the time. We'd all sit down to the table to eat and after Daddy said the blessing, Cousin Les would say, "Lord, have mercy upon us, keep our neighbors from us, for if they come upon us, they'll eat our rations from us." Remember that delightful old English night prayer, when we'd go to bed we could hear him say, "Lord lay me down to sleep, chinches and fleas begin to creep; if they bite me before I wake, I pray the Lord their jawbone break." It goes without saying that all of us in the house went to sleep with laughter in our hearts.

He was such an involved and active member of our household that it was easy to forget that he couldn't see. Case in point: My brothers use to love to ride their bicycles all the time. Our house sat beside the highway and Daddy was very adamant about them not riding their bikes in the road. One day Cousin Les was sitting on the front porch shelling peas and Mickey and Bob were riding their bikes in the yard. My brothers were always pulling pranks on Cousin Les, like setting off a firecracker next to his chair or moving things around on his dresser. One time they put Easter egg dye on his toothbrush, and for a couple of days his teeth and whole mouth, including his lips, were a bright green. We tried not to laugh, but it was one of the funniest sights you ever want to see. When he found out why we were all laughing, he just laughed too -he would just go along with them and laugh too. But rest assured, sometimes he would do something to get back at them. This was one of those times. On this particular day, as soon as Daddy came home from work, Cousin Les told Daddy that the boys had been riding in the road on their bikes. Daddy called the boys to him and confronted them about it. Of course, they denied it with pleas and cries, but to no avail. Daddy took off his belt and began to give them both a good whipping at the same time. Mama heard all the hollering from inside the house and came out to see what was wrong. She asked Daddy why he was whipping the boys and he replied, "Les told me them boys was riding them bicycles in the road and that's why I'm giving them a beating." Mama was astonished and she yelled at Daddy, "Carson, you know Les can't see; he's blind!" Daddy was so taken back that he just dropped his belt and said, "oh that's right." I tell you right then, my brothers were a little hot under the collar with Cousin Les but not for long `cause he was such a likable fellow that he just made you feel good to be around him.

Cousin Les was mighty scared of ghosts or "haints" as old folks use to call them (course Grandma called them "ain'ts" cause she said "twerent" no such a thing). He said he knew when a "haint" was in the room with him because he could feel the hair on his head stand up. He was especially nervous and uneasy if someone he knew or someone who lived close by had died. He said he heard their ghost come into the house and pass by him and knock something off a table or a picture off the wall. He wouldn't go to bed by himself for a few days but then, he'd eventually, get all right.

He had an old harmonica that he kept in his shirt pocket. He could make that little thing almost talk. We use to sit on the porch at night in the Summer and listen to him play the sounds of a train coming down the track. It sounded so real, you could almost see the train coming right up to the front door.

HITTING CLOSE TO HOME

1.	A home is a house with a heart.

2.	Even if you are in darkness, you can light up someone else's life.

3.	If you get a whipping for something you didn't do, take it in stride. You more than likely deserve it for something you had already done.

4.	Here's a new one for you: "Believe half of what you hear and none of what someone else sees."

5.	Sooner or later, your pranks catch up with you.

6.	Dead folks can't hurt you, but they sure can make you hurt yourself.

7.	Some folks can see more things in the dark than others can see in the light.

CHAPTER 9

Aunt Nee: A class act

My Daddy was born near Whiteville, PA. and later moved to a city called Ducane, near Philadelphia, PA, where he attended grammar school; then he moved with his parents to a small town outside of Charlotte, NC called, Bessemer City. His mother passed away when he was twelve, and his father (my Grandpa) remarried a very big-boned, tall lady who we thought was real mean. That woman would fry two chickens and eat every piece all by herself.

My Daddy had a sister that was born with a birth deformity. Her legs were crisscrossed under her like one sitting Indian style. Because they could not be straightened, her legs grew short and slender. Her upper torso was bigger and more expanded than that of a regular sized person her age; she would get around by walking on her hands.

Anyway, Daddy said that their new step mama was not very good to them, especially towards Aunt Nee. Aunt Nee did not require any special attention or special assistance because she could take care of her own needs. She bathed herself, went to the toilet by herself and combed her own hair. She climbed up on chairs and sat down and put herself to bed at night. What's more remarkable than the above was that she made beds, swept floors and got on a chair at the sink and washed dishes. She always wanted to do things around the house to help and she felt so good about what she could do.

What made Daddy so mad was that his pappa would let that woman treat Aunt Nee in such a shabby way. He said my step Grandma would fry chicken and give Aunt Nee only the head and feet to eat. Every time I heard that said it made me so sad, and I would go off by myself and cry my eyes out. So, at the age of thirteen years old, my Daddy ran away from home and got a job in a logging camp in Sampson County. He vowed that when he got married and settled down, he was going back home to get his baby sister. And it wasn't very long after he and Mary Florence married that she came to live with them.

My Aunt Nee was truly remarkable. She had been through a lot of hurt and pain that would have emotionally crippled some of us for life --but not her. When she was about ten or eleven years old, my Grandpa put her in the circus as a side show oddity. She was with the Barnum and Bailey Circus. They billed her as, "The Frog Girl". She used to captivate the family for hours as she told about the places she had been and the different people she had met. It was an adventure to her, but I hurt so deeply inside for her because her own pappa made money off of the way she looked. As a little girl, I could just imagine cold heartless people jeering and poking fun at her and it would break my heart. Mama always said and I quote, "I won't nothing but a bucket of tears".

My Daddy and Mama felt the same way too and I believe that it had caused a distance between Daddy and Grandpa. I loved my Aunt Nee so much because she was always happy. She laughed and played with us young'uns just like she was one of us. She loved to play dolls with me and she and I would sit on the porch for hours and color in our coloring books. She was not allowed to go to school because of her "seeming" disability, so as a first grader, I taught her the ABCs and how to count. My brothers and sisters helped to teach her how to print her name, but we never really taught her how to read beyond a few little words. I never understood why we didn't go further with her education. But back in those days it was easy to think that she would never have a need for it being handicapped as she was.

She loved to watch TV and she knew all the ad jingles by heart. One of her favorite tunes was the Frosty Morn Pig song, which advertised Frosty Morn Bacon. She really loved that song and would sing it constantly. You could hear her sweet voice ringing through the house singing, "The height of a piggie's ambition from the day he is born, Is just that he'll be good enough, To be a Frosty Morn. So let everybody join in, and sing it over and over and over again, Frosty Morn, sing it over and you sing it over again, Frosty Morn." She sang it around the house all the time especially when she was by herself. She had a beautiful singing voice and everyone enjoyed listening to her sing.

Mama made us little dresses out of pretty cotton print material, and she would make Aunt Nee's dresses too. Aunt Nee's hair was very silky and very long, and on Sunday Mama would let her wear it to church hanging down her back. Almost every Sunday they would ask her to sing a solo, and the whole congregation would stand up and just clap for the longest time when it was over. Then she would have to sing another selection.

I'll never forget this one particular Sunday they asked her to come up and sing. She loved to sing the old hymns and gospel songs more than anything else in the world. But this Sunday when they called upon her to sing, she must have forgotten what she was supposed to do or where she was for a brief moment. Everyone got really quiet waiting for her to sing. Suddenly, she started to sing the Frosty Morn Pig song. Well, the entire church broke out in laughter, and she realized what she had done and laughed with us too. Needless, to say, she composed herself and went on to sing; "The Lord Will Make A Way Somehow", and brought the house down.

I have never in all my days of living, met anyone with a sunnier demeanor or a more positive outlook on life than she had. She always smiled. She always had kind words to say about everybody and she never

45

ceased to praise the Lord for everything. Seeing her inspiring zeal and her enthusiasm for life was a pleasure; it was pure joy in itself to be around her.

SOARING ABOVE THE CIRCUS CALLED LIFE

1.   What is a freak? What is a human oddity? SOMEBODY'S CHILD.

2.   The heart of a child loves in spite of, but the spirit of that love must be nurtured.

3.   Eating two fried chickens at once exceeds the recommended daily allowance of fat for one person.

4.   A vow motivated by true love is always paid.

5.   And on the sixth day God created bacon; let us rejoice and be glad in it.

6.   The measure of a giant is not in height but in stature.

CHAPTER 10

<u>Our weekly trip to town</u>

Whether it was Summer, Winter, Spring or Fall, we all went into town on Saturday afternoons - the whole kit and caboodle. There would be young'uns sitting on grown-ups' laps, young'uns sitting on young'uns laps, almost hanging out the car windows; but we were all in there heading to town. Sometimes we would go to Benson, NC and sometimes we would go to Dunn, NC. It didn't matter to us young'uns where we went, just so we went to town.

Believe you me and rest assured, we all had truly *earned* the money Daddy would give us that week by working on the farm --even the littlest young'un.

In the Spring we pulled tobacco plants for planting, planted corn and soy beans and then planted the tobacco plants. Sounds like a lot of planting doesn't it? Well, it was. In the Summer we suckered the tobacco, planted cotton, chopped cotton, picked peas and beans, picked cucumbers, de-wormed tobacco (you really don't want to know), and toward the end of Summer, we started harvesting the tobacco. When Fall came, it was time to finish with the tobacco harvesting and start picking cotton. Of all the jobs on the farm that I had to do to help my family make a living, I hated picking cotton the worse. We would grade the cured tobacco and get it ready for the market. When the weather started to get cold, we would dig sweet potatoes and send them to the market. Everyone in our household worked.

Even though my brothers and sisters were older than me, Daddy still collected their week's wages from the landowner the same as he did mine. He would in turn give each of us some spending money for town. None of us ever complained because that was just how things were done and it was natural for our Daddy to have the say so over the family's finances.

As the baby of the family, I naturally got the least amount, but I was thrilled just to have money to spend. I was about eight or nine years old when I began to earn wages from the farmer for my work. I remember getting paid thirty-five cents an hour when I first started. My Daddy went to the farmer and reasoned with him that my work was at par with the others and that I should receive fifty cents an hour too; the farmer agreed. So after working hard all week just like the others, my Daddy would give me a dollar and a quarter on Saturday. You would have thought he had given me fifty dollars from how happy it made me.

We would head for town about 2:00pm in the afternoon. Once we got there everybody would go their separate ways. Of course, I had to hang with one of my sisters, but that was all right. The first thing we did was run to the "hole in the wall" where we could buy hot dogs. We were not allowed to enter through the front door, so we had to enter from the rear or stand at the back door and order. This didn't bother me much, because that was just the way it was, and I didn't know enough at that time to be upset about it. Life was good for me as a small child in the fifties and it didn't matter to me whether someone thought I was inferior or not. I now know that because of the love that was in my family, I grew up loving people no matter who they were, no matter their color or how they acted.

Now, after I bought 2 hot dogs for 50 cents (back then, they were 2 for 50 cents); a big cold Pepsi in the bottle for 15 cents, I still had sixty cents to spend at the Five and Dime Store. That store was like a wonderland filled with rows and rows of shiny, tinkling, twinkling, jumbled, "stuff' just to mesmerize young'uns. I would spend at least a couple of hours in there going from aisle to aisle, "oohing" and "aahing."(I knew better than to touch anything, `cause my Mama told me not to pick up "nothing" unless I was going to pay for it.) Most of the time I would buy a beautiful gold ring with a huge jewel on it and a jeweled bracelet or a pretty colored necklace with baubles all over it. I would drop quite a bundle in that store, about thirty five cents. I would always get Aunt Nee a pretty ring too so we could look alike.

You better believe --I guarded that last quarter with my life. I had to get the most out of it. About

5:30pm, one of my sisters or brothers would start rounding everybody up so we could head home. My last stop on the way to the car was at Walgreens' Drug Store. There I would get the biggest cone of Butter Pecan Ice Cream you have ever seen, and with the few pennies that were left, I would get soft peppermint candy.

I loved the sights, sounds and smells of town. It was such a treat for me and I thought it was the greatest place in the world. But there was one incident that took place that over shadowed my experience for many years to come.

My oldest sister's boyfriend, we called him Brown, was in the supermarket with her and our Mama while they were buying groceries. The rest of us were sitting on the hood of our car watching people walk by. We saw the sheriff's car pull up real fast and park in front of the supermarket. The Sheriff rushed in with his black jack in his hand. All of us ran to the door and windows of the market to see what was going on. In a few minutes, the Sheriff came out with Brown in handcuffs. My Mama and sister were crying as they followed the Sheriff outside. Daddy came running up and asked Mama what was going on. She told Daddy that one of our cousins was at the front of the checkout line and Brown went up to her --teasing her about getting in line ahead of someone else. There was a white man in line who made a nasty remark to

Brown and called him that "no no" word. It looked as if he and Brown were going to "come to blows" with each other. The man also accused Brown of looking at his wife in the "wrong way" and claimed that he brushed up against her in passing. The Sheriff was called by the owner of the store and Brown was arrested. I looked at Brown as the Sheriff brought him out of the store and he had a face of stone. That scene will stay etched in my mind forever. He was taken to jail and had to spend the night. Daddy bailed him out the next morning. He said the woman's husband already had a dislike for Brown because he wouldn't stop in the store aisle like a servant and let him and his wife pass by 'like they were the "King and Queen or something'". Nothing ever came of the matter again; we think the market owner went to the police and told the truth, so the matter was just dismissed –no charges were ever filed. You see, our family had been "trading" with this store/the owner for many years, and the owner thought very highly of my Daddy and Mama. After the incident, however, we no longer did business or traded with this store again; we started our buying in another little town close by, so consequently, the Saturday trips to town didn't hold as much excitement for me anymore. I guess for the first time in my life, I really grasped what being colored in the south was all about.

I tell you, what was even more of a life lesson to me many years later, after my sister and Brown were married and settled into their home, an old looking man on a very dilapidated truck knocked at their door selling vegetables. He did not recognize them, but they knew immediately who he was. He was the same hateful man from the supermarket. And, you know what, they never let on that they knew him but graciously bought fish and vegetables from him for many years. They said that just by looking at his sad countenance, they knew the Good Lord had already settled the score, and that was enough. What a powerful lesson in forgiveness for a young person to see!

COLORING OUR WORLD

1. Everything that glitters ain't gold.

2. It doesn't take a lot of money to have a good time; a little will do if you know where to go.

3. Young'uns will see the world the way the world is and the way others are by how you portray the world to them.

4. Be careful who you step on, they may have to give you a leg up in life.

5. "Vengeance is mine, saith the Lord; I will repay!"

CHAPTER 11

Playing house under the house

Our house was a big house with only five rooms, a porch that went all the way across the front of it and one that went three fourths of the way across the back of it. Like a lot of houses out in the country, it sat high off the ground either on cinder blocks or brick columns. It was high enough that I could almost stand up under it at age seven or eight --and I was considered a tall girl for my age.

My Daddy and the boys kept it swept out underneath, so it was real clean which made it easy to see what was under there. It was one of my most favorite places to play. I would take cardboard boxes under there and pretend they were my stove and icebox. Broken dippers from the water bucket became cook pots and lids from jars and snuff cans were my pans. Popsicle sticks worked great as spoons and forks. All I needed was a big pork and bean can full of water and I would make mud pies under there all morning long right by myself. Well, not exactly by myself. I had my doll baby and a stuffed teddy bear or two that by brothers won at the county fair.

In my make believe world there was always something to do. Meals to cook, young'uns to feed and send to school, clothes to wash, dresses to make, dishes to wash, and babies to rock. My Mama always knew where to find me when I got missing --under the house playing house. There was a daddy (husband), in my world, but he was always in the field working until it was time to eat or drive the pretentious car. Then we'd go in to town and buy some candy and come right back home. As I got older in my make believe world, I became the mama and the school teacher.

Of course, at the end of the day, every real person in the house had to sample my under-the-house gourmet creations, and of course, they raved about how good they were. From the earliest memories of my childhood, all I wanted to be was a happy homemaker. You see my pretentious house always stayed clean; the dishes would be washed in a matter of seconds; the baby very rarely cried; the food cooked up without much effort; the young'uns ate; went to bed; and went to school – that's it and nothing in between. The daddy of the house was hardly ever seen (Probably 'cause I couldn't decide whether he was Sky King, Ricky Ricardo, The Lone Ranger, Zorro, Ozzie Nelson, Spin or Marty.) Yes, these were ideal conditions for a play life.

In the Spring I'd go down to the garden and pick green peas and pull up some onions for me and my guests. Maybe a few wild strawberries that grew along the ditch bank, that is if I wasn't too scared. What made me scared was that one time I stepped

down in the ditch to pick some pretty wild flowers
that were growing on the other side; I stepped right on
top of a Water Moccasin. I told you I was fast! I
jumped back so quick that it didn't even have time to
strike. It uncurled and went down in the muddy dirt.
Of course it scared me and I do believe I scared it too, I
think. Needless to say, I dreamed about it for months.
I hate snakes to this day.

PLAYING FOR LIFE

1. In the house! Huh, I'd rather be under the house.

2. Pretending doesn't keep the commodes clean.

3. Babies cry, pee pee and poop --for real!

4. Just think – we deal with athletes feet, basketball practice, bills, car pools, couch potatoes, daycare, dentists, Eve's curse, fat burners, girdles, homework, insufficient funds, juggling schedules, KP all the time, leaving home, many chores, noisy kids, one day at a time, peer pressures, quarrels, responsibilities, standing anyhow, temptation, unending workdays, vamps and tramps, working full time, working part time, working all the time, ex-spouse, and Zantac.

5. And God created snakes! Why?

CHAPTER 12

Aunt Nee and Uncle Bud

For real though, there is someone for everyone. Who would have thought that my Aunt Nee would find love and happiness with a man? It never crossed any of our minds.

There was this family that moved in a house not too far from us that had a lot of children and sundry relatives that came to live with them, just like we did. One day they were passing our house and noticed Aunt Nee sitting on the front porch. Several days later the father of the house stopped by to talk to her. Well, as it turned out, he had a cousin that had a handicap too, and he thought that his cousin and Aunt Nee would be excellent company for one another. So my Daddy agreed to let him bring his cousin over on Sunday afternoon to meet Aunt Nee.

I can hardly describe to you my first encounter with "Mr. Bud". As an eight year old, I was completely dumbstruck; Aunt Nee was just another member of our family and she seemed perfectly normal to me. So I was totally unprepared for seeing Mr. Bud. He was head, trunk, and foot in that order. He was a little shy of a yard tall, with a very prominent head (not overly large but seemingly eye catching, nonetheless). He had no arms, but a small finger that grew out of his left shoulder. He had a stout body with no legs. On the left lower side of his body was a small foot that was turned outward. Can you imagine everyone gazing, with their eyes nearly bugging out? You could have cut the silence with a knife.

The cousin rolled this little man up to our porch and dropped him off. And the moment he opened his mouth, I knew even as a child that this was someone who was confident and sure of who he was. There was no mistaking the fact that he was extremely smart and he had a lot to say. Within a few minutes he had put us all at ease and guided us in accepting him without pity. I truly believe that something good was awakened in me on that day and that good has remained a part of me ever since.

You talk about an amazing man! This man was amazing beyond belief. He worked in the tobacco warehouse in Smithfield, NC, grading tobacco with his foot, and was paid a regular wage just like every other worker there. He was very mathematically gifted but had never attended school a day in his life. If you put a pencil between his toes, he could write his name in cursive as good as most people. My Mama said he really had a good head on his shoulders for business too. Because of my age, I didn't care too much about those qualities, but I did like the fact that he chewed tobacco and could spit a stream of tobacco juice further out in the yard than anybody I knew. Besides, he looked so cute the way he scooted on his butt to get around.

Mr. Bud must have been close to forty years old when he started coming to see Aunt Nee. They hit it off with each other right from the beginning. We all thought it was so cute; the two of them sitting out on the porch on Sunday afternoons dipping snuff and carrying on with us young'uns. I believe the only one that had any reservations about it was my Daddy. He was a little suspicious of the whole relationship. Not because he didn't want Aunt Nee to have companionship; I believe he loved her so much that he did not want her to be a victim of any hurt or ridicule. Also, Mama said that he thought Mr. Bud's relatives had a hidden motive for wanting to get them together. He felt that they wanted someone else to care for Mr. Bud the rest of his life. Even though he was very capable in many ways, he still needed assistance to perform the basic everyday functions in life.

Early one Saturday morning Mr. Bud's cousin and his wife came to our house and asked Daddy if they could take Aunt Nee out on a day trip with them. At this time Aunt Nee was about thirty years old, but Daddy still treated her like one of his young'uns. Daddy said it was all right with him and Mama, so they took Aunt Nee with them. It was late Saturday night when they brought Aunt Nee back home with some news that almost caused my Daddy to blow a gasket. Aunt Nee and Mr. Bud had gotten married ! I had never before --or since then --seen my Daddy so furious. We thought he was going to kill somebody. Mama was saying and doing everything she could think of to calm Daddy down.

My Daddy loved his little sister so much, and the marriage almost broke his heart. He was sure that her husband's relatives had maneuvered the whole thing. He could not understand how the system could legally marry two handicapped people like them. He insisted on seeing the marriage certificate, however, he still was not quite satisfied when he saw it. Mr. Bud's relatives had taken them to Dillon, SC, and because Aunt Nee was over twenty one years old, she did not have to have anyone's permission to marry. Back then, poor uneducated people did not know anything about annulments; if they did I'm sure my Daddy would have tried for one. But, such as it was, he just accepted it and tried to make the best of it.

Aunt Nee went home with Mr. Bud that night, and I cried so hard my eyes were swollen the next day. I was afraid that things would change between me and her, and I was jealous of her having someone else to love besides us. But I had no reason to fear. My Aunt Nee and me only grew closer to each other as the years passed, and Mr. Bud became one of the family. Daddy finally accepted him and even became very fond of him.

Would you believe that in about a year after they were married, they rented a house in Smithfield and took to keeping house --right by themselves. Of course, someone came and cooked for them every day, helped with the cleaning that Aunt Nee couldn't do, and assisted Mr. Bud with going to the toilet. They lived many long and happy years together until his death. After he died, Aunt Nee came back home to live with Daddy and Mama.

Sometimes I close my eyes and can see me and Aunt Nee sitting on the porch laughing and playing hand games. Oh what a beautiful world this would be if there were more Aunt Nees in it!

LOVE AIN'T ABOUT LOOKS

1. Beauty really ain't what you see, but what you feel.

2. Some matches ARE made in heaven.

3. Slow down and look around you, or you might miss something good.

4. Sometimes what seems so bad at first can turn out to be so great.

5. So, you don't have what a lot of other people have, use what you got!

6. Confidence and self-assurance don't come from what you have, but from how you see yourself.

7. Love WILL make a way.

CHAPTER 13

Help me, Holy Ghost!

"Chiren," churching, and chastising just seemed to always go hand in hand when I was little. My peoples were "holy rollers" from way back, and they did not shirk from it one bit.

I learned very soon in life that when God was talking, I was not supposed to. When God was moving, I was not supposed to be. When God was doing whatever it was that He was doing, I was not supposed to be doing anything that I wanted or had to do --even to the point of restraining my normal bodily functions.

"Chiren" in my church were definitely seen and not heard unless you were singing in the young people's choir or it was your Sunday to say a Bible verse in front of the whole congregation. Other than those occasions, we knew when to sit still and be quiet. Oh, it was all right if we dozed off to sleep as long as we were quiet about it. But there was no way that you could go to sleep in my church unless you were a drunk that hung out all night Saturday night and your wife made you go to church Sunday morning. The "goings on" inside that little place was enough to wake up a comatose person.

We attended a very small white cinder block church in town, that sat directly behind the railroad tracks. This made for very interesting acoustics every time the train passed through during our worship services. The loud sound would drown out all the speaking and music going on inside the church. Of course this never annoyed the preacher, the choir nor the congregation –not one little bit. They just kept on praising, and he just kept on preaching just as though the deafening racket wasn't even happening.

My Daddy and Mama, like everyone else, were oblivious to everything around them when they were "having a Holy Ghost filled time in the Lord", except when it comes to what their children were doing. They may have been praising God with their eyes closed, but believe you me, they knew exactly every minute what their children were doing --especially me. My Mama would make me go to the outhouse at the back of the church as soon as we parked on the grounds so I would have no reason to get up once I was inside the church. Sometimes she would allow me to sit beside other children I knew, with a warning that I was not to talk for any reason or move around needlessly. Daddy and Mama sang in the choir every Sunday so they sat at the front of the church on a slightly raised platform; with this view, they could look directly at me --no matter where I sat in church.

Twasn't long after the service got started that things would really get to jumping, and I really mean jumping. People would be jumping up and down in time to the music, hollering out stuff like, "Amen" and "Hallelujah"; "Praise the Lord"; "Preach it"; "Tell it"; and "Gloray". The women would jump so hard (it's called 'shouting') that their hats and even "earbobs" (earrings) would fly off. They'd shout right out of their shoes. Sometimes they would get so overcome by *the Spirit* that they would faint and fall out on the floor. Other folks would get down beside them and fan them until the Holy Spirit was finished having His way. And if it was a woman that was "slain in the spirit", then another woman would spread a white cloth over her legs so you couldn't see up under her dress. But the rest of the folks would keep right on rejoicing, right on shouting. Boy, I sure loved this part. It was so funny to see all those grown folks carrying on like they were crazy. But mind you, I was smart enough to laugh in a way that my Daddy and Mama didn't know I was laughing. `Cause you didn't laugh at God's people --no matter how funny they were.

Some of the people would start talking in strange sounding languages which was kind of scary to a young'un. My Mama said they were "speaking in tongues, as The Spirit gave them utterance". It just sounded like gibberish to me. I dearly loved the music though. It was so lively and so energetic. Everyone could stand up and clap their hands and keep time to the beat with their feet. It was glorious! Those people could sing like nobody's business. There was an old "hand me down" piano that always needed tuning, but that didn't matter because the lady that played it could almost make it talk. We had someone that played the guitar and the drums, and lots of women brought tambourines to shake. When the train wasn't passing through, you could hear the sounds from the church for blocks. I thought, even as a young'un, that this must be what heaven will be like.

Unfortunately, I didn't always listen to what my Mama told me. One such time was a Sunday that we had some new folks to visit our church. Me and their little girl hit it off right away and we begged to sit together in church. This request was granted, along with the obvious admonitions. Things were going along just great until my new friend wanted to get up during the preaching to go to the outhouse. Naturally, she could not go by herself, and I was too embarrassed to tell her that I was not allowed to move from my seat. So, laying my own better judgment aside, and hoping that my Mama was too engrossed in the preaching to notice, I got up from my seat and almost ran out the church beside my little instigator. (Big mistake! Huge mistake!) We were half way around the building when I looked up and there stood my Mama. Lord Have Mercy! Help me Holy Ghost!

"What did I tell you", she said, "about getting up and moving around when service is going on"? By this time, my partner in crime had split --nowhere to be seen. I could not say a single word. I knew my Mama and I knew what was about to happen. She reached out and broke a long keen switch off the hedge that grew next to the church, took me to the outhouse, and went to town on my butt. Afterwards, Mama returned to the choir stand through the side entrance and I returned to the church through the front door, moving much slower than when I went out. I found where my Grandma was sitting and sat down beside her, laid my head in her lap, and promptly went to sleep. The incident was never mentioned again, and the incident never happened again.

That's one time that the Holy Ghost, whom I knew to be my Helper, did not help me at all.

LET THE CHURCH SAY AMEN

1. Jump up and praise the Lord sometimes. It will make you feel good and praising will keep the "nodders" awake.

2. The Holy Ghost is not a warden over your actions.

3. Don't be so quick to ridicule the "foolish looking things" for the Lord; He uses these to confound the wise.

4. When somebody tries to get you to do what you are not supposed to do, you better stop and think about it. It can have a "painful end" result.

5. When the "saints go marching in," some of them will have switch marks on them.

6. If you can "Huckabuck" for the devil, you sure ought to "cut a step or two" for the Lord.

7. When you see disturbing actions of some folks' young'uns' in church on Sunday mornings, don't you wish switches still grew right beside the church?

CHAPTER 14

Saturday night, country style

Saturday night was the one night that I got to really stay up late, even though we all had to get up and go to church the next morning. There was this local television station that used to broadcast a local show at 10:00PM called Saturday Night Country Style with Jim Thornton. It had to be the funniest show we had ever seen. I don't believe that it was meant to be a comedy, but a variety show featuring local talent. It was sort of a cross between The Ted Mack Amateur Hour and The Porter Wagoner Show. It was a hoot! The host wore bib overalls and talked real "country". Most, if not all of his quests were just plain old down home folks with not much talent but a lot of guts.

There was a real big boned woman who used to play the harmonica and she never wore any shoes. She had the biggest and longest feet you ever did see. The whole time she was playing the harmonica, the camera was focused on her feet while they supposedly kept time with the beat. There would be banjo picking and fiddling, square dancing, and some really awful singing. I'm sure by now you have guessed that it was a country and western show. We young'uns loved to get up and imitate the singing and dancing, making it as funny as we could. By the end of the show, we would all be laughing so hard, almost to the point of tears.

While all this craziness was going on in the front room, Mama and Grandma would be in the kitchen cooking Sunday dinner. My Mama always cooked Sunday dinner on Saturday night because we stayed in church so long on Sunday that she said she was not going to spend all day Sunday cooking. So when we'd get home from church, all she had to do was warm up dinner and put it on the table. My Mama was a smart woman. She didn't have a lot of education, but she had a great deal of "mother wit." Usually, while she was cooking, she would prepare something special for us while we watched television, and that was usually hot dogs. Saturday nights were the only time my Mama ever made hot dogs. Even after eating them in town that afternoon, I was eager for one of Mama's. We always had mustard, onions and chili to put on them. A many a time though, she would fry fresh Croakers (fish) and make hush puppies. Um Um good!

There was this real scary horror show that came on after the "Saturday Night Country Style" show called "Nightmare". My brother's wife and I were the only ones that loved to watch it. We would get a quilt and sit on the couch, turn off all the lights and sit there right up against each other, all the while being almost too scared to breathe out loud. Lon Chaney as The Wolfman, could make the hair on the back of your neck stand up. Frankenstein seemed human enough, because little children in the picture were always drawn to him. Of course he usually drowned them or something, 'cause he didn't know his own strength. I "kinda" felt sorry for him. The one that I least liked to watch was Bella Laghosey, as Count Dracula. Those hypnotic eyes use to haunt me in my dreams.

All in all, it was still fun. Right after the scary show was over I would run and jump in the bed and pull the cover up over my head; Saturday nights were amusing to me.

I'll never forget the first time we saw an all black cast on television. It was on the Kraft Theater. The production was called, "Green Pastures". It was all about heaven, the angels and all the singing and dancing going on up there. We were all glued to the set. Nobody dared to visit the outhouse until the program was over. None of us thought anything about black folks being stereotyped or portrayed in negative ways. It was just plain good entertainment. The program made you feel plum good and happy inside.

FAMILY FUN NIGHT

1. Today it's hard to watch television with your young'uns, because you don't have enough hands to cover their eyes and their ears at the same time.

2. There is a vast difference between laughing at people and laughing at people (with people). Get it?

3. I got rhythm, you got rhythm, but some of God's people didn't get rhythm.

4. If you eat fried fish at 10:00pm and watch a scary movie at 11:00pm, you won't know which one gave you the nightmares.

5. Folks nowadays have lost sight of who they really are 'cause they're too busy trying to be everybody else.

   Be what you are, and live the life God gave you!

CHAPTER 15

Pigs, pork chops and tears

My Daddy was a very honorable man. He was respected by black folks and white folks, alike. His main concern was providing a good home for and feeding his many young'uns and family members. So, it is a natural conclusion that he raised pigs.

We had a big pig pen way down at the back of our house. It was mostly my job to help feed them before I went to school and after I came home from school. I didn't mind this job too much because I got to watch the little pigs playing around and drinking milk from their mamas. Those little pigs were so cute. I use to give them names too. Mama kept a bucket in the kitchen that she would throw scraps and leftover food into; this was called slop (although with all us folks in the house, there weren't very many leftovers). Daddy bought big bags of feed from the FCX store to mix with the slop. This mess looked bad, but the hogs didn't care. We would give them ears of corn fresh off the stalk because Daddy said it was too big and too tough for us to eat. Sometimes Daddy told me to pull up these long weeds that grew at the edge of the yard and give them to the hogs along with the slop. We called these hog weeds.

It is so easy for a young'un to get attached to people and animals. I loved those little pigs and the sows (mamas), and the "bo" hogs (papas) too. When they would see me coming toward the pen, they would all run up to the fence. Deep down I knew it was because I was bringing them food, but in my child's heart, I believed it was because they just knew it was me coming to see them. They would just be squealing and trying to outrun each other to get to the trough. Whenever and each time you put food before them, they would eat it. While I was feeding them, I would sing a song to them by Stevie Wonder. The words to it went something like this:

Oh would you rather swing on a star
Carry moonbeams home in a jar;
You'd be better off than you are,

Or had you rather be a pig?

A pig is an animal with dirt on his face

His shoes are a terrible disgrace;

He has no manners when he eats his food,

He's fat and lazy and extremely rude;

So by the way if you hate to go to school,

You may grow up to be a pig!

With all that feeding and loving, it didn't take long for those cute little pigs to grow into full sized hogs. And you know what that meant; sausage, pork chops, ham, spareribs, neck bones, souse meat, pigs feet, liver hash, pig tails, cracklings, pork rinds, chitterlings (chittlin's to country folk) and whatever else you could get from the pig. Mama said that we ate everything from the hog except the squeal. I loved most of the stuff that came from the hogs, but I sure hated the way you had to get it.

As soon as it got cold enough, usually sometime in January, my Daddy and the other men in our family would start preparing for a hog killing. Even now, it's hard to think about it. They would start early in the morning just after the sun came up. I can close my eyes and still picture all the black wash pots in the yard with fires lit under them. It would be so cold you could see your breath in the air. There would be long tables set up in the barn to cut the fat for cracklings and lard.

As soon as I saw my Daddy and the men heading toward the pen, I would start crying and pleading with them not to hurt the hogs. I would cry so hard that I would almost make myself sick. My Mama would make me go into the house to be with Aunt Nee. My poor Aunt Nee would comfort me the best that she could, but I would just clamp my hands over my ears so I couldn't hear the hogs squealing, and cry that much harder. Finally, after an hour or so, I would get all right and go back outside.

Mama and the women folk had the joy and pleasure of cleaning the chitterlings. They would be a good piece away from the house out in the field. If you have ever smelled chitterlings then you know why they were far away from the house. If you've never smelled them, you ought to get down on your knees right now and thank God! Even the buzzards would fly south at chitterling cleaning time. Of course Mama and the women folk would make me tote water to them so they could wash them out. Hated it! They would wash the chitterlings so clean that the guts would almost be white when they were finished. They would use the real thin chitterlings to stuff sausage in. Mama never cooked chitterlings in the house, 'cause they smelled just as bad when they were cooking as they did when they were cleaning them. She would cook them in one of the big black wash pots in the yard.

After all the messy work was done, like cutting up the meat, drying out the cracklings to get the lard, cooking the skins to make the pork rinds, then Daddy would salt down the slabs of side meat, hams and shoulders for preserving. He had his own meat grinder and he would grind some of the meat and fat and add seasoning to it and make link sausage. By this time, it would be getting toward dark and time for supper.

Mama and the other women would have long since gone into the house to cook supper for everybody. And what a supper it was! We always had fried pork tenderloin with gravy, rice, turnip greens, baked sweet potatoes, hot buttermilk biscuits, some kind of fruit cobbler and that "yucky" liver hash mess that all the grown-ups loved and we young'uns wouldn't touch.

You know, I must have been a crazy young'un, 'cause I thought if you carried a greasy lunch bag to school that meant you were poor. For lunch, we took things like pork chop sandwiches, ham biscuits, sausage biscuits, tenderloin biscuits, fatback biscuits, and homemade apple or sweet potato jacks. Mama always put a little jar of fruit she had canned in the lunch bag too. I would trade my lunch with one of the town young'uns that always had old dry peanut butter and crackers, or a sandwich with a thin slice of bologna and a little bit of mayonnaise. Of course we carried bologna sandwiches too sometimes, but with lots of Kraft Mayonnaise, courtesy of the Kraft Theater commercials. My lunch was always better than theirs, and the town young'uns would fall all over me to get me to exchange with them. When I did eat my own lunch, I was so ashamed that I would put the bag right up to my mouth so no one could see what I was eating. (Foolish, huh!)

You let one of them fat fully packed biscuits cross my path now; I'll eat it so fast it'll make your head swim.

THE FOOD CHAIN OF LIFE

1. The yearnings of the stomach are stronger than the yearnings of the heart.

2. When po folks ate them they were pigs feet, pig tails and pig ears; now they are Gammon Trotters Fricassee, Le Pork Bootee Au gratin and Pork Orinthol with Rosemary.

3. If you want to make friends, walk around with a bag of homemade crispy fried hog skins (pork rinds to you squeamish folks).

4. The pig, lowly esteemed, but comes highly recommended.

5. Enjoy the life you have and don't desire the lives of others, for what you have is better than what you think they have. Your life could be ham, and theirs could be bologna!

CHAPTER 16

<u>Doctor Sniffer, M.D.</u>

I believe that young'uns have been playing "doctor" ever since the world began. That is the one game that everyone can play, `cause all you need is an imagination and a willing patient. My sister, Sudie Mae and our friend Ricky and me played this game every day of the week when we would get together. It didn't matter which one was the doctor and which of us were the patients; we just played and had a grand ole time.

Ricky was a great playmate who always shared his candy and goodies with us, however, I have to admit, that even as a child, I thought him a mite weird. His hair was as red as a fox's tail --at least that is what my Mama said. He was so pale that you could see all of his veins through his skin, even in his face. He was a puny boy who had hardly any meat on his bones at all. Sometimes he would be sick for several days and could not come out and play at all. But when he did come out, he was full of mischief.

There was an old abandoned tobacco barn behind our house that we played in all the time. We would take cookies and other goodies in there; Ricky would bring goodies from his house too and we would have tea parties. Ricky's mama and daddy didn't mind him playing with us all the time because there was no other young'uns his age around to play with.

He was a few years older than me, but about the same age as my sister Sudie Mae. When we played "mama" and "daddy" I would always have to be the baby. We would play all day long until his mother called him in to eat supper. Most of the time she would have to come over and get him because he did not want to go home.

I remember two incidents that threatened our innocent relationships and almost caused irreparable harm. One occurred when we were playing doctor. This role playing usually consisted of one of us listening to the heart of the other two --with an instrument made from a string with a little metal bell (the little top cap from a Christmas tree ornament) hung on the end of it (a make believe stethoscope); we would pretend to take pills (using jelly beans) that the doctor gave us, and having our ears and throats looked into.

But on this particular day, Ricky got a little bit more curious about my sister's anatomy. You see my sister had this big "outie" (a belly button that looked less like a button and more like a knob), that just happened to be hanging over the waistband of her shorts. Well, as usual, we went to our favorite spot to play, when doctor Ricky decided that he could examine the "outie' better if he went into the house and got his daddy's magnifying glass. So he did. He had just stretched the patient out on one of the old burners in the barn; he bent over her to get a closer look when his mama came into the barn. Lordy, she

threw a plum fit when she saw what she thought --
him looking at my sister's "thang."

Good gracious alive! I thought she was going to
burst into flames. Her face got red and you could see
the veins jumping in her temple. She grabbed Ricky
by the collar and almost slung him through the barn
door. She yelled at us to go home and said she was
gonna tell our Daddy and Mama what we were doing
when they came in from the field. Me and Sudie Mae
didn't understand why she was so upset or what we
had done wrong, but we knew if she told Daddy and
Mama anything on us, we were sure to get a
whipping. True to her word, as soon as they got home
from the field, here she comes, dragging poor Ricky
behind her. My sister and I started crying as soon as
she came up on the porch. We could already feel the
fire that Daddy was gonna bring to our britches.
Ricky's mama made him tell the whole story; this is
when she found out what he was really doing. None
of us got a whipping that day, but Ricky was not
allowed to play with us for a long time.

Remember I said that Ricky was a little weird.
Well, this should convince you of that. His daddy
would park the tractor on the lot between our house
and theirs --after using it in the fields. For some
unknown reason, Ricky got it into his head to take the
cap off the gas tank and sniff the gas fumes. He
started doing it almost every day. He tried to get us to
do it but our Daddy had told us not to be on that
tractor. It got so that Ricky was sniffing that gas
longer and longer each day. After he did it for quite

some time, he began to have a real wild look in his eyes and he appeared to have less energy; in fact, he didn't want to play anymore like we use to. He made us promise him that we wouldn't tell anybody and by being young'uns, we didn't know the danger in what he was doing.

One day he was sniffing the fumes when nobody was around him, and he passed out. His mama found him and they rushed him into town to the hospital. He had to stay in the hospital for a very long time. Our family was so sad because we all thought a lot of that crazy boy.

When he came home, he was never quite the same. Even though we played together, we didn't have as much fun as before because he was always tired a lot and he couldn't keep up with us as well as before.

Our family moved from there pretty soon after that, and I never saw Ricky again, but I thought of him often through the years. I wouldn't be surprised right now if Ricky owned a filling station somewhere.

HOW TO SHATTER INNOCENCE

1. If you play doctor long enough, you'll want to examine things more closely.

2. Strange belly buttons make for heightened curiosity.

3. Grown folks really can make a mountain out of a mole hill.

4. If your mama and daddy tell you not to do something, it's best not to do it, even if everybody else is doing it.

5. Your nose can get you in a heap of trouble.

6. If someone is hurting themselves, tell somebody. You might lose a friendship, but you might save a friend.

CHAPTER 17

<u>Grandma, I was just play coughing; I don't have a cold, really I don't!!!</u>

You know what they say; "What won't kill you will cure you if there ain't much ailing you." Sometimes you would have rather died. The stuff old folks use to make "chiren" take for their ailments would be considered young'un abuse today.

I d-double dare you to sneeze around my Grandma Sudie; and heaven forbid if you coughed! She would take down a big ole deep tablespoon that she kept on the mantel piece and pour in it to the very brim the most vilest, disgusting mess ever to be forced upon poor innocent, trusting young'uns. If you have never tasted castor oil, you should be on your knees thanking the good Lord right now! But, to really make it intolerable, she would heat the spoon over the stove to warm the oil. Meanwhile, I'm standing there trying to figure out how to faint before the oil was ready.

She would call me to her and demand that I open my mouth real wide. Then she would pour that oil in my mouth. Automatically my stomach was coming up to meet my throat. The little swallowing mechanism at the back of the throat just plain refused to work. So there I was; could not swallow it and dared to spit it out. That's the true meaning of agony. As I am standing there, with castor oil still in my mouth, well, it seemed as if time just stood still too. Grandma finally decided that one of us had to do something, so she would get "smack dab" in my face and say, "swallow that stuff gal, right this minute and I mean it." Lord have mercy on me! I would throw my head back as far as I could git it, without falling backwards, and let that thick, greasy, foul smelling mess ooze painstakingly slow down the back of my throat. "Good googley moogley!" I think a tablespoon full turned into a pint. My stomach wanted to block it, but it was as scared of Grandma as I was. As soon as I finally swallowed it, she would shove in my hand a chunk of peppermint candy or an orange with a hole punched in it. This was supposed to cut the oil's after taste, or either it was an apology for what she had just done to me. All I know is that it didn't work. Many hours later I would burp and the horrible taste would come back in my mouth. If you thought it was bad the first time, it was ten times worst the second time around.

She even had the nerve to drop a few drops in the mole (soft spot) of my head, to "help run the cold out." Believe you me, the castor oil in my belly did not need any help running the cold out. In about thirty minutes after I took it, I had the "back door trots," or you may know it as "the runs." Everything in me that was not attached to something else in me came out so much, that my shoes were always too big for me the next morning.

(REMEDIES FOR WHAT AILS YOU)
AND, YOU STILL LIVING, IN SPITE OF

1. FOR COUGHS

-A teaspoon of cane sugar with a few drops of kerosene or turpentine in it. Course, this will surely guarantee that you win the prize for face contortions. -A tablespoon of lard with salt sprinkled on it. (Takes gagging to an art form, another level.)

2. FOR WHOOPING COUGH OR THE CROOP
-Get a mess of green pine needles, a hand full of kucka burrs and some rabbit tobacco (rabbit you know what). Add to a pot of water and boil to make a tea. Sweeten with honey and drink it hot, "often". (Note: To get to "often" you have to live through the first time.)

3. FOR A SORE THROAT
-Make a tea from the bark of a Red Oak Tree. It is so bitter! It will turn a saint into a sinner.

-Shhh! Don't read this one out loud. I don't know if anybody ever did this, but there was talk going around that you could *"make water"* and gargle with it and that would cure it just like that. Anyway, that was the talk going around.

4. FOR CUTS

-Go in a barn, look in the corner and get a palm full of cobwebs. Put them in the gash and while you're holding the person down, pour turpentine in the cut. (Cover your ears 'cause cuss words are coming.) Bandage with strips from a clean white sheet. I bet you this is how jitter bugging got started.

5. FOR A BOIL

-Take a knife and run it through cold ashes in the fireplace. Use the back of the knife to mark an "x" across the boil. Cover the boil with a clean white sheet strip. (Seems like folks back then wore more sheets than they slept on.)

6. FOR A FEVER BLISTER

-Put earwax on it! Yuck! Hey, it's cheaper than Blistex.

7. FOR A TOOTHACHE

-Rub some whiskey or white lightening on the gums. After a few treatments of this during the day, you should sleep good at night.
-To pull a tooth, tie one end of a string around the tooth then tie the other end around a doorknob. Tell the poor nervous as a cat young'un to look the other way and slam the door! You might have done better by tying the young'un to the chair first. (Now, close your eyes and picture that.)

8. **FOR POISON IVY**
-Take a bath in a tub with a little Clorox in the water. You probably won't come out a shade lighter, but if you kept your underwear on the skid marks would be gone.

9. **FOR NOSE BLEEDS**
-Drop metal spoons or keys down the person's back. (How this works? Your guess is as good as mine.)
-Tie a bow around the index and middle finger. (Anybody's guess is better than mine.)

10. **WHEN YOU JUST CAN'T DO NUMBER TWO**
-Trim a piece of soap and push it up the "shoot". When it starts to blow bubbles, you know relief is on the way.

CHAPTER 18

Wonder woman lived at our house

My Mama, Mary Florence, was some kind of woman! There was not anything that I thought she couldn't do. She has always been my heroine, even when I didn't know what the word meant. It just seems to me that young'uns back then used to live and have a reverential awe of their parents; they used to have respect for them; you know, you would be astonished and amazed of your parents then, but not today. Wonder why that is?

Anyway, my Mama's face should be beside the word "mother" in the dictionary. Now of course she ain't perfect, but a young'un don't know that. She use to say that very thing; "Lord I sho ain't perfect, but I do the best I can." And that she did! She'd get up with Daddy every weekday morning before daybreak. You could hear Daddy stroking the fire in the wood stove and smell Mama's coffee all over the house. Then you would hear the clanging of pots and pans and cooking stuff. She just didn't cook what you would call a normal breakfast meal; no siree, and you talk about a hearty breakfast, WOW! She would fry side meat, pork chops, sausage, fritters (country pancakes), eggs, grits and made from scratch biscuits. She'd mak,e about three lard stand lids of them biscuits. Them biscuits would be so good, they'd make your tongue slap the back of your head. Everybody ate about three of them apiece. That woman could sho nuff cook, and she never skimped on the butter and lard.

You are probably thinking to yourself --why in the world would she cook so much food! Well I'll tell you why. You see country folks ate three times a day. They worked very hard in the field so they had to eat to keep their energy and strength up. Mama didn't have a lot of time to devote to cooking so she would cook a lot of things in the mornings and just add vegetables to them at dinnertime and supper. That's how it was done back in those days.

In the Summer she would cook a huge pot of them little new red potatoes. We grew them in our own garden. You didn't even have to peel them. We'd put them in a tin tub of cold water and let them sit for several hours. Then we'd take our hands and swirl them around in the tub. The thin red skins would shed right off. She wouldn't cut them up either --she cooked them whole. Out of the pot she'd pour them into a big ole ceramic bowl and set them on the table. We young'uns would run in when she wasn't looking and stick a fork into one of them taters and throw it in our mouths. Man oh man, you talking 'bout hot! That tater would almost burn the roof of your mouth out. Course, it was a small price to pay for something that tasted so good.

Don't even get me started talking about her desserts. I declare her cakes were all of ten inches tall. That chocolate yellow layer cake was out of this world. She would let us lick the batter bowl and spoon and we would almost go to blows with each other over who got the chocolate frosting bowl. It just seemed like anything and everything she cooked was the best in the world.

Mama didn't seem to mind having a lot of kin folks around all the time either. We didn't have the kind of folks that cussed and raised sand all the time. Most of them were just plain ole fun loving, hardworking kind-hearted people. It seemed like all our friends were our kin.

On Sundays after church we'd have a yard full of cousins playing dodge ball, baseball and horse shoes. The women would bring dishes of food from their houses and add it to our Sunday dinner. There were so many of us that we had to eat in shifts. Boy that was some kind of fun! The children ate after all the grown people ate. Sometimes if you managed to get a piece of fried chicken, it was the "part that went over the fence last". That was the chicken's hind part. You know, the little butt section with the oil bag on it. If that person was you, you were a mite disappointed 'cause you had waited all week for fried chicken. Now mind you, it wasn't that we didn't have chickens; there were chickens galore running around in the yard, but it was just that you only had chicken for Sunday dinner and no other time during the week.

Monday was always wash day, except we could not wash sheets between Christmas and Old Christmas (January 6). Grandma Sudie said that it was bad luck to wash bed clothes at this time. It meant that someone in the family would die. Mama didn't believe it, but she would not go against her mama. You can't begin to imagine how many loads of wash we had on wash day, my word!

We didn't have a washing machine back then. The way we washed wasn't too far advanced from the way Daniel Boone's wife washed, at least that's what I thought. We used two big black cast iron pots with hot water for washing the clothes and two tin tubs of cold water for rinsing the clothes.

Daddy and the boys would get the fires under those big pots kindled and roaring hot. Mama had taught all us young'uns early on how to sort clothes by colors, so there would be big piles of sorted clothes on the back porch from each one of the dirty clothes' storage places in the bedrooms. Mama would begin by boiling the bed sheets and white clothes, then she'd lift them out and put them in a pot of soapy water. She would take this big wooden paddle that Daddy made for her and push the sheets up and down and around and around, "sorta" like the motions of the agitator in a washing machine. Next, she would put the sheets over in the first rinse water that had something called "bluing" in it and let them stay for a while. After this they would go in to the final rinse. Meanwhile, this process was repeated with the other laundry. She would wring them all out by hand and then hang them on the line. Those white clothes were so bright that they looked like they were gleaming. People were always telling Mama how pretty her white clothes looked on the line. It usually took all day to wash the clothes, even when we young'uns were home to help. Unless the clothes had to be taken off the line in a hurry from the threat of rain, my

Mama always folded them as she took them off the line. That is something that we all do to this day, now that we are all grown. Even though washing was an all day job, Mama always fixed dinner, every day, and it was always ready when Daddy came home from the field at 5:00pm, then later on we would have supper.

My Mama was a great organizer and administrator. She had a job for everyone in the house to do and she made sure that it got done. The older girls basically kept the house clean, while the boys helped Daddy with the yard work and the outside upkeep of the house. Both Mama and Grandma Sudie did most of the cooking and my oldest sister would help too. After dinner, Mama would comb our hair every night and braid it tightly so it would look nice and fresh for school the next day.

I don't ever remember wearing a wrinkled dress to school in my whole childhood. Every Saturday morning Mama would get out the iron and the ironing board and iron all our clothes for the upcoming week. On Fridays, she would take the special clothes -- like Daddy's and the boys' Sunday shirts and our Sunday dresses and starch them with Argo starch, sprinkle them with water, put them in a clean pillowcase and put them in the refrigerator. These clothes would iron so stiff that they could almost stand up by themselves. Mama took such pride in her ironing, and she was especially finicky about not having "cat faces" on our clothes.

I can remember seeing her sitting at her old Singer sewing machine making pinafores for us girls out of white organdy.	Mama would make little gathered dresses from the flowered sacks that Daddy would get flour in, for the pinafores to fit over. My oldest sister Lois was the only one of us girls to learn how to sew from Mama. Frankly, I hate it then and I hate it now.

My Grandpa Tom and Grandma Sudie lived with us because Grandpa was run over by a hit and run driver while he was walking along a street in town.	The accident left him with almost all of his limbs broken. He was placed in a body cast from his chest to his ankles. This made it extremely hard for Grandma Sudie to take care of him by herself so they moved in with Mama and Daddy. Grandma Sudie was a mite feeble too so she needed to be where someone could look after her as well. Mama and Daddy did, along with all their little "chiren" and sundry kinfolk. For over a year, my grandpa was in that full body cast and he had to be turned over at least three times a day. Daddy and Mama would turn him in the mornings before they left for the fields, come back at dinner and turn him, and then turn him again before supper. Just before they went to bed at night they would turn him again. They did this every day -- the whole time he was in that cast. Besides taking care of a bedridden father, a sickly mother, a very ill daughter, a puny preemie and six other needy young'uns, Mama had to work in the fields to help make ends meet. Why she never lost her mind or just walked away was a mystery to me until I was old enough to realize from where and from whom she drew her strength and endurance.

There was always singing in our house and my Mama was always doing it. She would sing the "songs of Zion" while she worked at any and all tasks. You could hear her in the kitchen, on the porch or out in the yard as she praised the Lord in song. Sometimes she would be singing and the tears would be streaming down her face. Yes, tears of joy but other times tears of tremendous burden. I know that now, and yes, it just makes me love her a thousand times the more. But through it all her faith in God remained constant and sure. I remember that when life's challenges became a little rough and tough for her, you would hear her singing these words," I will trust in the Lord, I will trust in the Lord, I will trust in the Lord -- till I die."

To me, my Mama was such a pretty lady. She had real pretty big legs. Back then, a woman that was full figured was thought of as a "fine specimen" of a woman. Folks used to say that a woman on the plump side was well taken care of. Mama never wore makeup of any kind, but had the softest, smoothest skin you ever want to touch. Mama didn't have a lot of time to worry and fuss about her looks, so God fixed it so she wouldn't need to.

Of all the people in the world (the rich, the famous, the glamorous, the ordinary), there is no one that I would rather be like than my Mama. There was a love inside of her that goes well beyond anything that you could touch or feel. She truly loved with the love of the Lord.

HONOR THY MAMA

1. Mamas will when others won't; Mamas do when others don't; Mamas can when others can't, and Mamas shall when others shant.

2. Mamas "make do" so her family won't have to.

3. If Mama didn't cook it, it ain't as good.

4. A Mama never airs her family's dirty laundry, unless of course it's gym socks.

5. A Mama works hard to iron out the wrinkles in her young'uns' lives.

6. Mamas don't come with a job description, 'cause there's no way to keep track of all they do.

CHAPTER 19

<u>Grandma Sudie and the devil snake</u>

My Grandma Sudie was a very small, frail looking woman. But honey chile; looks can be so deceiving! That little woman was about five feet, two inches tall, full of pure spit and fire. You would know that too if she ever got a hold of your behind.

After Grandpa Tom died, Grandma Sudie remained with us instead of going back to live by herself. Of course Daddy and Mama never entertained the thought of letting her live alone. Back then, folks took real good care of the aged and ailing members of their families in the home, no matter what they had to do to do it. My Grandma was just like my Mama and Daddy to us young'uns; whatever she said --we did. Grandma was not shy or timid about "chastising" us young'uns either. Disobeying her for not doing what she said was something that never entered our minds.

But like all grandmas, she would let us get away with stuff that Daddy and Mama wouldn't and she would "pet us up" after we had gotten a whipping from either of them. She would always find a way to sneak us a piece of candy or chewing gum to make us stop crying. She kept Juicy Fruit Gum in her pocket book all the time. Today, when I smell that Gum, it brings back delicate and delightful memories of Grandma Sudie.

Behind our house, way back down in the woods was an old irrigation pond. Around it was sort of swampy and overgrown, which made for snake paradise. Big ones, little ones, all colors and sizes. I hate snakes! Okay, I said it and I mean it! I hate snakes! Daddy would not let anyone kill the black snakes `cause they kept the rats away and he said that the king snakes were good because they would kill other snakes. But to me, the only good snake is a dead snake!

There was no grass in the yard around our house and Daddy and my brothers kept the yard swept clean at all times. This made it easy to see if there was anything crawling about. We never saw any snakes in the yard or close to the house, but we would find them in the barn, the chicken coop, and sometimes in the pig pen, which would just about scare the living daylights out of me. But not my Grandma. When she saw one, she would take the hoe and chop its head off. It didn't matter what kind it was to her; a snake was a snake. She didn't care how big it was either; she would immediately attack it with the hoe.

There was this one time though, when I saw her backing away from attacking a snake. One afternoon, about the beginning of Summer, all the women folk and young'uns were sitting on the front porch shelling garden peas. Daddy and the bigger boys were working up at the tobacco barns. There was a beautiful field of wheat growing and standing very tall across the road in front of our house. All of a sudden, Mama stood up and pointed toward the wheat field and said, "What in the world is that coming this away -- parting that wheat like that?" Well, everybody's attention immediately became centered on that object moving slowly but steadily in our direction. We could actually see the wheat part and crush down to the side as it cut a path about ten inches wide through the field. By this time, we were all huddled around Mama and Grandma on the porch, too mesmerized to even breathe out loud, much less breathe at all. Grandma said it so softly you could hardly hear her, "Lord, have mercy, that's a snake!" She shouted out, "One of you young'uns bring me the hoe!" By now the snake had reached the end of the field and was moving toward the road. If I live to be a hundred and twenty years old, I don't believe that I will ever see a snake that big and long again in my lifetime. You can just imagine what he looked like to a nine year old child. He looked like the inflated inner tube of a car tire, but over fifteen feet long, with a head the size of two big fists. His skin wasn't shiny black, but dull gray and old looking.

Grandma Sudie grabbed the hoe and ran into the road to meet the snake as it crossed the ditch. I had never seen anything like this before. There was so much snake that it was in the road across the ditch--

and part of it was still in the field. As Grandma raised the hoe to hit it, it actually raised up and began to strike at her. Do you think this made her back off? No siree! That little woman brought that hoe down across that snake's back again and again. It sounded like something hitting hard rubber. She was using so much force that she broke the handle of the hoe in two, then she yelled for a bigger hoe all the while never missing a lick with the broken one. Before one of us could get the second hoe to her, the snake dropped back down to the ground and headed back into the wheat field. We young'uns ran to the ditch and threw rocks and stuff at it, but it just casually took its time and went back into the field. We never did see its tail. We watched that snake go back into the field and when it got about mid ways it curled up; y'all, that snake was about three feet high above the wheat.

Grandma said that it was not a real snake because she couldn't kill it and because it was so big. She said it had to be something from the devil. So we always called it the "Devil Snake".

When Daddy and the boys came home, we told them about the snake so they went into the field and the woods looking for it, but they didn't find it. Strangely enough, no one else had ever seen that snake before, and as far as I know, no one has ever seen it since.

AGE IS COURAGE PROVEN AND STRONG

1. Remember, old age is where you are heading, live long enough and you will get there.

2. Real strength doesn't come from the muscles, it comes from the mind.

3. Fight the good fight and fear will flee.

4. Watch as well as shell peas, for the devil rears his ugly head when least expected.

5. Snake stories are like fish stories; they get bigger each time you tell it.

CHAPTER 20

"Grandma, the school bus left me!"

Tell me this. How does the school bus leave you when it has to turn around in your yard because your house is the last stop on its route? The answer --when you plan it that way --of course.

At the age of eight, I was in the second grade because my birthday came in November and I couldn't start school until I was seven. So this made me a year behind. Well, that really does not have anything to do with the story so I will move on.

My first year in school was so wonderful. I can close my eyes now and see Mrs. Ward and the classroom. If I concentrate just a little, I can even remember what my classroom smelled like. The walls were a bright yellow and there were pictures and cutouts all over them. There were small writing desks for everyone with places to put their lunch bags and notebooks underneath. I loved school so much and could hardly wait to get there. My teacher loved all of us and hugged and kissed us often. She made us mind too and would not hesitate to use her paddle if she had to. My Mama said I could "pick up things real easily" and that's why I did so well in school.

Life was great --until I hit second grade --and Mrs. Blank Blank, I might add. She was my first experience with prejudice from someone of my own race. You wouldn't believe how she treated the "poorer," and yes I am forced to say, "darker" young'uns in her classroom. If your Mama or Daddy was a teacher or someone who seemed to have an "uppity" kind of job, then you were considered special, and if you were light skinned with nice hair", you were almost worshiped by this obese, red headed, freckled faced colored woman. It was a rude awakening for a seven year old young'un who unfortunately, did not fulfill but one of the requirements to be treated with dignity. I had "nice hair". Yipee!

I got so tired of getting up giving someone else my seat because they wanted it. I got so tired of raising my hand to answer questions but was never called on. I couldn't understand why my teacher never sat at my table during lunch. Why wouldn't she ask me to carry the lunch money to the office sometimes? How come I never got to pass out the pencils or crayons? Did she always have to look at me (with 'that look') like that? What had I done to be so ignored?

I was so unhappy! But I was scared to tell Daddy and Mama because I thought they would say I was making it up. In those days, "chiren" didn't "bad mouth" grown folks like they do now, even if there was cause to do so. So I figured that I would handle it my way. I just wouldn't go to school.

A young'un's mind is a wondrous place of simple solutions. My plan was so easy to carry out and who would ever be the wiser? The bus would always come after Daddy, Mama and the boys had gone to the field. (On days when Mama didn't go to the field, I wouldn't pull my little stunt.) When I heard the bus coming over the hill, I would run outside and hide behind the barn or "high tail" it down to the outhouse. The bus would pull into the yard and turn around. My sister, Sudie Mae, would get on the bus and the bus would blow its horn again and again for me. After a little while, I would hear it pull out the yard and start back up the hill. Then I would sprint from behind the barn and run into the yard yelling for the bus to stop, knowing full well that the driver could neither hear nor see me. There was nothing left to do then but go into the house and pretend that I had been in the outhouse when the bus had initially arrived -- and that I could not quit what I was doing, so the bus left me. Poor Grandma was a mite puny by then and usually was in the bed this time of the morning so she didn't know that I was "telling a tale." By the time Mama would come from the field to fix dinner, I would be happily playing with my doll baby or under the house making mud pies. But, on this one particular occasion, she came back to the house early to check on Grandma and found me still there. She made me go to the field and get Daddy. Daddy hurriedly put me in the car in an attempt to catch up with the school bus and put me on it. Daddies and mamas think they are smart, don't they? Trust me -- you can't fool them for long. My missing the school bus happened a few more times before the big day of the "showdown".

Daddy had plowed the field beside our house that Monday and it had rained all night long that night. Tuesday morning dawned with gray skies and an over cast, with a hint of drizzle in the air. I heard the bus coming over the hill; it was time for me to go into action! Out of the house I ran, headed around the back of the barn. Just as I turned the corner, who should I run smack dab into --the body of my Daddy. Oh Lordy Lordy, what do I do now! There was nothing to do but head out across that plowed muddy field, with him right on my heels. Unbeknownst to me, Mama was in the house and still in her nightgown. Mama yelled to the bus driver to wait and hold the bus for me. Then she took out across the field after me too. Picture this: A little girl, with a lean body and extremely skinny legs, with long pigtails standing straight out behind her as she is running --running with all her might, miring up in mud to her thighs, as a grown man (my Daddy running in slow motion) is chasing her. To complete the scene, a woman with a long nightgown on and a head rag tied around her head, is tripping and falling in the mud trying to catch this "po mud crazed young'un." Wouldn't you know it! Them young'uns on the bus was enjoying this side show!

I was fast, but not too smart, or at least not as smart as my Daddy. The farther I went up the field, the deeper the mud got. Finally, I had so much on my shoes and my clothes, that it weighed me down and that's when Daddy caught me. He picked me up, all the while me kicking and screaming, and carried me right to the front door of the bus. Y'all, that man carried me onto the bus and sat me in a seat. I was a pure wreck. My socks, shoes and legs were plastered with mud; there was mud spattered all in my hair and my clothes were filthy. He told the bus driver that whatever else he did, do not let me get off of the bus 'til it reached school. I was absolutely mortified! No one on the bus said a word to me the whole way to school. I sat next to my cousin who was in high school and who watched me like a hawk so I wouldn't try to run for the door every time the bus stopped at a crossroad. It was amazing how quiet that ride to school was. You would have thought that the other young'uns would have been laughing and picking at me, but they weren't. I guess I looked too pitiful sitting there making those jerking motions. You know the kind you make after you have cried so hard and your body is trying to settle back down. By the time I finally got to school, I was completely worn to a frazzle.

As a child, I didn't know nothing else to do but to go to my classroom. I can remember how my heart was so heavy for a little girl. But I went on in there anyway and took my seat at the back of the room. Students were just getting off the buses, so many of them did not see my filthy appearance. I put my head down on my desk to keep from looking at anybody, when I heard my Mama's voice asking for me. I looked up and at the front of the classroom there stood my Daddy and my Mama. My beautiful Mama walked over and took me by the hand and led me out of that room into the girl's bathroom. In her arms she held a big bag, which had a clean dress, clean socks, clean underpants, a slip, hair ribbons and my black patent leather Sunday shoes. She took a wash rag and a piece of soap out of her pocketbook and began to wash and clean me up. There is no way I can ever describe to you the love that poured out of my heart for my Mama that day. She told me not to cry anymore because she and Daddy were there to find out what was wrong and why I hated school so much. You know, after I got older and looked back on that incident, I realized that Daddy had to have pushed that car to the maximum speed to get to the school at the same time that I did. They did not want me to be ashamed or made fun of by the people at school. When we came out of that bathroom, I was beaming like a light bulb.

My "ole" mean teacher stood out in the hallway and talked to my folks for a very long time that day. At the end of their conversation, Mama walked back in and kissed me on the cheek and said she would see me when I got home; she even gave me a dime and a quarter so I could buy lunch from the cafeteria. (We young'uns always brought our lunch from home.) I felt like I was really somebody special that day. It's truly amazing what a visit from your folks can do. Even the "high falutin" young'uns wanted to talk and be with me after that. But the greatest change was in Mrs. Blank Blank. She actually started calling on me in class, and she would let me run some errands for her to the office and the lunchroom. I never knew what my Daddy and Mama talked about with her, but whatever was said, surely did change her attitude; not only toward me, but toward the others in class like me.

There were some more highlights in the second grade and one of them was the time we performed in the school's Spring music festival. It was so thrilling! I remember that our class did a dance to "Tiptoe Through the Tulips", (before Tiny Tim). We girls wore pretty little costumes made out of yellow and green sheer fabric with real full skirts. My Mama made mine.

By the end of that second grade school year, I was in love with school again; in fact; Mrs. Blank Blank and I actually became fond of each other--for real.

SCHOOL OF LIFE

1. Prejudice comes in all colors, shapes and sizes, but however it comes, it hurts somebody.

2. Daddys and Mamas are not as dumb as you think.

3. The right word, placed in the right ear, by the right person, can right a grievous wrong.

4. "From the outhouse to the schoolhouse"; sounds good enough to put in a speech.

5. You can run but you can't hide, and if you run in mud, you will slip and slide.

CHAPTER 21

"Mama, please don't let them put that dirt on Grandma!"

Whether death is the act of the soul leaving the body and going up to heaven, or whether it is the body going to sleep for eternal rest or whether the Lord wants you with Him because He likes you, all I know for a child, death is hard to understand.

Grandma Sudie's health began to steadily decline by 1960, and she had to go to the doctor's a lot. She was even in Duke Hospital for a spell. By this time, my older sisters were married and had moved away from home. Jay Bird was married also and they lived up a piece near the field from us. After Grandma came out of the hospital, she really needed nursing care. Mama taught us how to help care for her. I remember learning how to change the sheets on Grandma's bed without her being out of it. I would gently roll her to one side, take the sheet from under her, roll her back to this side and take that part of the sheet from under her. Then I would repeat the same process when putting on the clean sheet. That was quite a chore for an eleven year old, but I did it with such pride. Mama had taught me how to be careful and gentle so as not to hurt Grandma. It's really amazing what you can do when you have to. When she didn't have the strength to feed herself, I would feed her. Sometimes I would crawl over in the bed beside her and just lie there with her while she slept.

You see, before Grandma's health started to fail, she had basically taken me under her wings and taken on the biggest challenges of my upbringing. Every Summer she and I would go and stay with my Aunt Annie and Uncle Ervin. They only lived about twelve or thirteen miles from us, but it was like going away on vacation. They had no children of their own so they loved for me to come so they could have someone to dote on for a while --and I just ate it up!

My uncle and his brothers were tobacco farmers of a sort; they were much "more well off" than we were. But that did not mean they spent a lot of money. They did not spend their money on luxuries either. It was well known that they squeezed a dollar 'til it hollered. But Aunt Annie and Uncle Ervin did live in a nice enough cinder block house. Of course, my aunt ordered curtains and stuff from the Speigel catalogs all the time, and my Daddy use to say that my uncle never paid more than five hundred dollars for a car in his life.

My days there were spent in playing with the young'uns who lived close by them. There was one little girl with whom I became especially attached and we were like Peat and Repeat. Although she was clearly the ring leader I was very content to follow. We played tea sets and dolls, Mama and Daddy, schoolhouse (she was always the teacher), and all kinds of make believe games. We even played Cowboys and Indians with the neighborhood boys. It was so much fun playing Hop Scotch and Simon Says, One Two Three Red Light, Mama May I, London Bridge is Falling Down, and Ring Around the Rosie. Not to mention Jack Rocks and Marbles. I could shoot a shooter as far as any boy. We would play at full blast as long as the sun was out. After dinner and a wash up, I would fall into bed, dog tired. Such were the days of Summer.

I didn't understand sickness or old age. All I knew was that Grandma couldn't do the things she used to do. People didn't tell young'uns a whole lot of grown up stuff in them days. I think they thought, the less we knew, the better off we were. Why burden a young'un with worries that they can't fix? We really had some good folks in our church and in our family. When they heard about her sickness, they started coming and bringing food for us.

Then one Saturday night, for some reason, our house was full of church people. They were singing and praying in the room where she was. The yard was filled with cars and young'uns. There were young'uns there that I had never even seen before. I was in heaven! In the midst of laughter and giggles of young'uns lost in a game of Hide and Seek, I heard my Mama's agonizing wail, "O Lord Mama, please don't leave me." Instinctively, I knew something had happened. I ran into the house just as Mama fell to her knees and laid her head on Grandma's lifeless bosom, sobbing her heart out. The dam seemed to break all around me as my folks and others began to cry and moan. Someone took me by the hand and led me out on the porch and sat me down with Aunt Nee. I put my head in her lap and cried for all I was worth. I don't know why I did; I think it was because everyone else was crying, especially my Mama, because I did not really understand what had just happened.

After a while Mama came out and put her arms around me and I hushed. It's hard for me to put it into words, but it almost felt like some kind of holiday or something. You have all these people around you, showering attention on every member of our family, I was so excited. The reality of what just happened had not sunk in.

Mama had brothers that lived in Philadelphia, PA and she needed to get word to them about their Mama. She also had to get in touch with the undertaker so they could pick up the body. I knew all this 'cause I was stuck to Mama like glue with every move she made. We didn't have a telephone and it was too late to wake up the people we worked for to use their telephone, so Daddy, Mama, me and a few others drove into town so they could use the pay telephone. I don't remember very much about the call 'cause I didn't hear them, but I sure do remember the ride back home. It was in August and the night had been very warm and very clear, 'cause we young'uns had played outdoors the whole night. While Daddy was using the pay phone, I noticed that a thick heavy fog had rolled in. It was so thick that it was white. We could not even see the store fronts as we rode down Main Street heading for home. I guess one could say it was as if the heavenly clouds were upon the earth. For some reason, it was a spooky feeling. Daddy said he had to drive about twenty-five miles an hour once we left town 'cause he could hardly see any distance in front of him. I remember seeing him hold his head out the window a few times, trying to get a better view. It was as if a veil of secrecy or grave clothes had been placed over everyone in the car, for no one was saying a word; like everyone was suppressed. We saw only one other car out driving that night, and its red tail lights cast an eerie red glare ahead of us in the fog. Maybe it was because I was young or maybe it was because of the circumstances, but that night stirred up strange feelings that I never before experienced --none that I can recall. Thinking about it even now still gives me goose bumps.

When we drove into our yard, most of the cars were gone. The house was shrouded in fog so thick that all you could see was a dim glow of light through the windows. It was a mite creepy! Once we were inside, I noticed that the mirrors on the walls had been covered up. I didn't ask why, I just thought it odd. When I went into the room where Grandma slept, I had expected to see her still on the bed with the sheet pulled up and over her face just like I saw the preacher put it before we went into town. But she was gone and to my bewilderment, so was the bed that she had died in. O Lord, that was the barest, emptiest space in the whole wide world. My Grandma was gone......

The next few days were a whirlwind of activity. We cleaned house like mad people. There were people in and out all day long. My Uncle Wilbert and Uncle Mack and their families came to the house. The house was busting at the seams with people night and day. There was so much food; food going to bed and some upstairs on the pallet, (ask anybody). There was so much going on that I almost forgot the reason why it was going on until late Saturday afternoon when we young'uns were out in the yard playing. This big, long gray hearse drives up in our yard and backs up to the front door. I was anxious to see what this was all about. These two really nice looking men got out and went into the house. Pretty soon a gray truck also pulls into the yard, and some more men got out. Once in the house, people started moving furniture around and even taking some furniture to other rooms. The men in the truck started bringing in tall floor lamps and folding chairs. By this time I was so nervous I felt like I wanted to throw up and I couldn't explain why. I think it was because I knew that something very unpleasant was about to take place, and how right I was. One of the men opened the back door to the hearse and reached in and turned some kind of crank. Slowly, a gray brocade casket began to slide forward into the waiting hands of the other men. Four men took the casket inside our house and into our front room amid a silence you could cut with a knife. They placed it on a steel looking stretcher with wheels on it, with a gray velvet skirt on it that reached to the floor. My insides were churning like mad. They pushed the casket in the corner and placed a floor lamp at each end. By this time everyone at the house was crowded into the front room. When the lamps were plugged in and turned on, they gave off a very soft pick light that cast a calm yet unnerving glow over the room. Then one of the men moved to the head of the casket and lifted the lid. There lay Grandma Sudie, quiet and still with her eyes closed and a slight smile on her face.

I could not move or even utter a sound. My eyes were transfixed on her, and I could hear my own heartbeat. "O Lordy Jesus, Mama", my older uncle half moaned, half sobbed. "No Mama, no", as he ran to the casket and nearly took Grandma Sudie in his arms. The other folks were trying to pull him away and comfort him at the same time. This triggered sobs and tears from everyone in the room except the undertakers and a few of us young'uns. We just were spellbound by a "real life dead person" in the house. After a while things calmed down and the grown folks went back to what they had been doing in other parts of the house. The undertaker came in and set up a stand with a book on it so people that came to see Grandma Sudie that night could sign their names on the book. Then he hung a big wreath with green leaves and white flowers outside beside the front door, so folks would know that someone was dead at our house. By late afternoon, the house was full, the yard was full and folks were still coming to pay their respects; at least, that's what Daddy called it.

That night when most of the crowd had left, I went into the front room to see my Grandma Sudie -- just to take a closer look for myself. They had turned all the lights off except the pink ones and had spread a pink piece of netting across the top of the casket so it covered her face. Her salt and pepper hair had been done up so pretty and she had on a white dress that looked so soft. Her hands were folded across each other on her bosom and she had white gloves on. They had put lipstick on her lips; I wanted to wipe it off cause I knew Grandma didn't think much of women that wore "paint" on their faces. But I was scared to. I figured I'd tell Mama about it the next morning. I kept looking at her chest, waiting for her to breathe...waiting and waiting –and waiting. Finally, later that night, my cousins and I slept in the room across from the room where she lay; I don't recollect closing my eyes all night long, 'cause I just didn't know what Grandma was gonna do. She had always told me that if I was bad after she died, she was coming back to give me a good switching and I knew she meant it too. She used to say to us young'uns all the time after she would catch us doing something when we thought no one was looking, "Every shut eye ain't sleep and every goodbye ain't gone." Maybe this was what she was talking about. Lying there peering at that casket brought to mind so many of the ghost stories that my brothers and sisters use to scare me with. I sure was one glad young'un to see the sun come up.

With the morning came a flurry of things going on. It was Sunday, but we didn't go to church. Everybody was running around getting dressed and ready for the funeral. There were still folks like flies at the house. I'll never forget the new dress I got for the occasion. It was a pink dotted swiss with short puffed sleeves and it had a ruffled crinoline slip that peeked out from the hem. I also got patent leather shoes and new white socks with lace around the top. Even on that woeful day, I thought I looked really cute. All the women were dressed in black, with black hats and everything, and the men had on black suits and white shirts.

The hearse and two long gray cars drove into the yard not long after dinner, (which is lunch for country folk). I can remember standing on the porch watching as the undertakers took the casket out of the house and put it in the hearse. The radio in somebody's car was playing, "Michael Row the Boat Ashore, Hallelujah", and it sounded so lonesome. That song will always

122

remind me of the day that I had to say goodbye to Grandma Sudie. We had to line up in the house by order of our kinship to Grandma. All who didn't want to drive could ride in the "family cars". Aunt Nee and I rode in the one with Daddy and Mama and Uncle Mack. Our car was in line directly behind the hearse as we went to the church. Folks meeting us on the road would pull over to the side and stop as we passed by. And I thought about how my Daddy always would do that when we met a funeral procession too.

When we got to the church, it was already packed out, except the seats that were saved for the family. They brought the casket in and set it right in front of the pulpit. There were more flowers around in the church than I had ever seen in my life. As we took our seats, I heard Mama whisper more to herself than to anybody else, "People sure thought a lot of my Mama." Hearing that just made me so proud of Grandma Sudie. At that point, the service took off. The choir started singing and people started clapping and praising The Lord. If you didn't know better, you would have thought you were at a revival meeting. Then the preacher got up and really stirred the folks up talking about heaven and how we all have to do what Grandma had already done. Afterwards, someone sung a solo and read some cards and stuff, then it was time to go to the cemetery. They put the casket at the back of the church and opened it up so folks could get one last look at her before she was buried. Several family members were so broken-hearted and distraught with grief and sadness; they needed individual attention and comfort, so they had to be looked after by the first aid lady who came with the undertaker. But not me; I was too busy looking to see if someone was going to pass out 'cause I remember one time I heard Mama say, "so and so" had fainted at such a one's funeral.

When we arrived at the cemetery, they put the casket over a deep hole on some metal bars with some straps attached to it. I was fine until the preacher started reading from the Bible and they started lowering the casket down into the ground. Then, I blurted out, "Mama please, don't let them put Grandma in that hole, please Mama, don't! She can't see down there. She can't get out of the box down there. Please Mama, stop 'em. Daddy, make 'em stop; she'll be scared in there by herself". I was crying so hard I couldn't see. The men came around and took the bars and straps away and begin to shovel dirt into the hole. "Oh God, please God I want my Grandma. Mama, please don't let them put that dirt on Grandma." I was begging and pleading with all my eleven year-old strength, but nobody was doing anything. Daddy was trying to hold me and soothe Mama too at the same time; he was having a hard time doing both. Finally, I pulled away from Daddy and ran to get back in the car with Aunt Nee; I laid my head on her lap and cried until my eyes hurt and they became swollen. She told me that Grandma Sudie was not really in that box in the ground, but that the Grandma I loved had already gone up to heaven to be with Jesus, and that the only thing in that box was a shell of her. She said that all the angels in heaven were rejoicing and happy to see Grandma and that she was having a good ole time. She was not sick anymore and she felt better than she ever did in her life. Aunt Nee said that one day I would see my Grandma again if I lived for Jesus, like Grandma did.

You know what --I believed her and I never thought about Grandma being anywhere else but up in heaven with Jesus.

LIVING FOR A BETTER LIFE

1. Raising young'uns is every grownup family members' job, if you want them raised right.

2. Young'uns don't need a lot of "things" to have a good time, just their imaginations.

3. Young'uns can understand responsibility, "if" you trust them with it.

4. We all fear what we don't know much about.

5. "Homegoings" are celebrations for those who are heaven bound.

6. When a situation seems so bad that you can't stand it anymore, look for the good in it and you will find peace.

7. This world is not our home, we're just passing through.

CHAPTER 22

<u>Faith, wisdom and a miracle</u>

My sister Shirley was a natural born housewife. Even as a young'un, I could recognize when someone was a good mama and a good housekeeper. She worked so hard in the field and in her home to make it right for her family. She married while she was in her teens and started having young'uns, one right after the other. Her husband worked on a chicken farm and the owner moved them into an old broken down place -- three boards shy of a shack next to the chicken houses. Actually, it appeared the chicken houses were in a much better shape than their house was. But she didn't complain; she just made the best of it. It's puzzling to me that when you are poor and uneducated, people think you don't have the same feelings or desires that they have. Anyhow, she and Jun seemed to be really happy together with what little they did have. At least it looked that way to me. I use to walk through the woods to their house every chance I could get. She always had something good cooked and I would help watch after the babies sometimes. When I stayed overnight, I always slept in the bed with them 'cause I didn't like sleeping in the other room by myself. They'd always tease me about how wild I slept. I'd start out at the head of the bed at night and end of at the foot of the bed in the morning. I remember when their first baby was about a month old, I spent the night with them. The baby was in a bassinet at the foot of their bed. During the night while sleeping, I kicked the bassinet over and the baby fell out. The baby slept through the whole thing, but I thought the daddy and the mama were going to have a fit; they were so overwrought, but all was well. Needless to say, I had to spend the rest of that night and all other nights in the spare room whenever I came to stay overnight.

My Grandma Sudie's sisters and their families lived in Burlington, NC; we would all go up to visit them a couple of times a year, mostly on a holiday or some other time like that. They lived in a big old barn looking house that sat up real high on cinder blocks. I mean it was way off the ground. It needed a lot of fixing up, but they couldn't afford to do it themselves and the landlord wouldn't.

One year, when my sister Shirley's oldest young'un was about two years old, our whole family carried food over to have Thanksgiving dinner with them. It was so cold that day. There was no hot water in their house, so water had to be heated on top of the big warm morning wood stove in the front room. That stove, along with the cook stove in the kitchen was the only source of heat for the house. Our cousin Henry would get that heater so hot that it would be fire red on the outside of it. And that was the way it was on that day. Red Hot! There was a bucket of water being heated on top of it to wash the dishes with. We young'uns were off playing in the back rooms somewhere, while the women folk were in the kitchen cleaning up; the old folks and men were in the front room around the fire.

Suddenly there was a tremendous sound, like thunder, and the whole house shook. People were screaming and yelling for us young'uns not to come in the room. I could hear my little nephew crying his head off. It took a few seconds for us to realize what had happened. The floor beneath the heater had given away, and the boiling water on the stove had poured out over on my sister's baby boy. The heater would have fallen on him too, if Cousin Henry had not caught it in his bare hands and diverted it away from the baby, as it dropped through the floor to the ground. Immediately the women folk took charge. They grabbed the baby and took his clothes off. A lot of his skin and flesh came with the clothes too. Little James Paul was burned from his waist down on both sides. The grown folks began to pray. Someone was sent to get a woman who could "talk the fire out". Mama and Grandma were barking orders for clean white bed sheets, linseed oil and other stuff. I loved that baby so much; my heart was about to break in two every time I heard him scream. Mama said that God was so merciful, because a short while later he drifted off to sleep. Someone was busy looking after Cousin

Henry's hands too, for they were burned terribly. Later, he said he didn't even remember catching the heater. He just remembered seeing the baby heading toward it as it started to topple over.

Pretty soon, Daddy and one of my aunts came back with a real light skinned freckled faced woman who took the baby into her arms and closed her eyes as she began to chant something. The room got deathly quiet. I make note of her skin color and freckles because when she finished doing whatever it was she was doing, her face was beet red, especially her lips. I have never seen anything like it. Daddy later said that she could, "talk fire out", because she had never seen or knew her mama. Another one of those mysteries that young'uns didn't understand.

No, they never did take the burned baby to a doctor. They did the doctoring themselves. I remember Mama and Grandma going over to my sister's house every day to change the bandages and put more of that homemade salve on him. He could not walk anymore and mostly laid around. To my recollection, they would take his wrappings off and let his burned places get air for a period of time. Then they would coat those burns with that salve and bandage him back up. They wouldn't allow him to be held a lot except by his Mama and them. My sister seemed very sad for a long time, but Mama and the other grown folks would encourage her as much as they could. There was a real good preacher lady that lived not too far from us. She would have Bible lessons in her house and we young'uns would go so we could get the cookies and Koolaid she gave us. Anyway, Mama said the preacher lady had the gift of healing, so she came over and laid hands on the baby and prayed. I never missed a chance to go with Mama to my sister's house and I was allowed to stay and help her sometimes.

It wasn't long before Little James Paul learned to walk again. His burned places healed so well that there were hardly any noticeable scars. He was a happy, laughing baby again. Mama said it was a miracle. She said that by all rights, he should have been scarred for life, but he wasn't. Today, if you look at the legs of this forty year old man, you would be hard pressed to find any evidence that the terrible accident ever happened.

You can't put a price on wisdom; you can't put boundaries on faith, you can't put limits on God and you cannot explain a miracle.

A HENPECKED LIFESTYLE

1. Which came first, the chicken or the egg? Silly question!

2. Ain't no lips big enough to "talk some landlords out of the fire" (h---, that bad place).

3. Folks without faith should be as rare as hen's teeth.

4. To make some omelets, you first have to break some eggs; hey, if you live next to a hen house, that ain't no problem.

5. What you lack in knowledge, you can make up in faith.

6. You can find strength in the time of need.

7. Who can repair something or someone better than the person that designed them? Nobody – nobody but God!

CHAPTER 23

Birds do it, bees do it –why can't wees do it!!!

I must say --I come from a really entertaining and adventuresome family. Them young'uns were always doing something that made you go "huh."

Right off the bat, there's my baby brother Bob, who's Christian name was Carson and who was indeed a piece of work. They said when he was about three years old, he did not like to wear clothes. Mama or my sister Lois would dress him and a few minutes later he would be running around buck naked. He was cunning too. He had found an old rusty pocketknife with the blade broken on it. He'd take the skin of his "weedle" between his thumb and forefinger, and pull it out in front of him and proceeded to use the broken knife blade like a saw to cut his "weedle" off. He'd yell to them as he made 'see saw' motions with the blade, "I gonna cut it off". Well I tell you, they'd start running toward him and he started running from them, just a sawing on his "weedle" with that knife and laughing his little head off. When they finally caught him, they would discover that he was sawing with the back of the knife the whole time. Mama would burn his bottom up and put his clothes back on and before the day was over he'd do it again.

He was also the same little boy that ruined Mama's Christmas cakes one year. We had a screened in porch on the backside of our house that served as a cold storage place for Mama's cakes and pies at Christmas time. Back in those days, the women folks would start cooking their cakes days before Christmas cause they baked so many different kinds.

Mama had baked one of each; a chocolate cake, a pineapple cake, a coconut cake, a German chocolate cake, a lemon cake, a black walnut cake, a chocolate pecan cake, an applesauce cake and several other kinds. It was just a couple of days before Christmas. She had been baking all night long and on into the next day. The cakes were put out on a table on the screen porch to keep them cool. Bob makes up in his mind that he didn't want to wait until Christmas to have some cake. So he pushes a chair up to the table, climbs up on it and commences to put his fist right smack dab through the middle of one of the cakes –then he pulls out a hand full and eats it. By the time he was discovered, he had done this to about half of the cakes on the porch. When Mama opened the door to the porch and saw what he was doing, she ran to him, slapped him down, picked him up in her arms, hugged him to her and started crying. He was crying and she was crying. What a sight, everyone would tell me. 'Course I was too young to remember this, but the story has lived on for years and years.

Bob just couldn't seem to stay out of trouble and he absolutely was the target of mishaps. There was this one time on a Sunday morning, when Mama had dressed him for church. (Repeat after me: THERE WAS NO INSIDE TOILET!) So Bob being Bob, has to run to the outhouse, just as they were loading up in the car to go to church. In a few minutes they heard Bob yelling. Daddy runs down there and "good gracious a live", Bob had fallen in the outhouse hole. How he managed to do that defies explanation. Anyhow, Daddy drags him out by the collar (because he couldn't comfortably put his hands much on any place else), and stands him up by the rain barrel beside the barn. Then he and the young'uns dash water on Bob until he is at least rinsed enough that they can take his clothes off. Poor Bob and his clothes are then put in the rain barrel, where Mama pours buckets of warm soapy water on them. Daddy and the rest of the family goes on to church while Bob is left at home to dry out.

Next we come to Bob's compatriot in crime, my knee baby brother, Mickey, whose Christian name is Thomas. This boy loves to pull pranks on folks. We had chickens galore running around in our yard. 'Course, by Sunday there were always two or three less than there was the Sunday before. Sunday dinner was not Sunday dinner without the "Gospel Bird" on the table. I later found out that the reason they called it that was because the preacher use to go to the home of one of his members every Sunday to cop a free meal,and he would eat more chicken than the law would allow. But let's get back to the story. With all these chickens in the yard, there was plenty of chicken poop everywhere. Have you ever seen chicken poop? Well it's brown and white and it comes out in a squirt. When it dries, well it just looks like little piles of dried poop. But to a three or four year old, I don't know what it looked like. That's how old my knee baby sister was when Mickey use to tell her that those squirts of dried chicken poop was candy. Sure enough she went for it! (Over the lips and pass the gums, look out belly, here it comes.) All good things must come to an end at some point, and the point of Mickey's end was at the end of Daddy's belt. You talking 'bout a whipping; Daddy tore his behind out of his frame, or so I'm told. I was too young to remember this too. I seemed to have missed all the good whippings 'cept my own.

But the caper to end all capers was the time that Mickey and Bob decided that they were going to *fly* over to Mr. Check's house, a neighbor, who was my uncle's brother. Anyway, I know what you're thinking, and the answer is "No." We did not own a Cessna plane, and my Daddy was not a crop duster. The only time Daddy ever flew was probably when he was "three sheets in the wind".

Here's a quiz for you. What does a chicken have that makes him fly? Right you are! And what's on

136

these wings? Right again! So my brilliant brainey scientific brothers concluded that all they needed to have, to be airborne, were feathers. So first they plotted the best place from which to make their take off. Wouldn't you just know it, the roof of the outhouse. Then they gathered up all the materials they would need, which was a passel of chicken tail feathers. You see, when you are undertaking a great journey such as this, you want those that you dearly love to experience this great exploit with you. Naturally, they chose to take the gullible, trusting, and totally naïve knee-hi baby with them. Even in their dumbness, they were smart. Other than the baby (me), Sudie Mae was the smallest and lightest person in the house. So she was an excellent candidate for the maiden flight.

Them boys took some old crates and stacked them up against the outhouse and the three of them climbed up to the roof. They proceeded to stick feathers in the waistbands and cuffs of their pants, around the sleeves and cuffs of their shirts, behind their ears and in their hair. They had so many feathers coming out from Sudie Mae that she looked like a plump, juicy, Holly Farms Chicken.

Once they were all feathered up, they were ready for takeoff. I did tell you they weren't stupid, didn't I? They pushed Sudie Mae off first, with the instructions to, "flap your wings". They figured that by her being light weight and little she could easily fly. And if she could fly, they could fly. I must tell you she went down like a lead balloon --bare feet and all --right on a broken bottle. Oh no! She started crying. Mama heard her and came out to see what was the matter. The boys were trying to scramble down from the roof and get to her before Mama did so they could remove the damning evidence. Did not happen!

Mama came. She saw what looked like a crying chicken with a bloody foot. She took Sudie Mae in the house and doctored her up. The boys were told, "Wait till yo Daddy gits home." Oh my my my! "Them there" is the most dreaded words a young'un would ever want to hear. Pretty soon Daddy comes home. My brothers had just about peed in their pants thinking about the killing they just knew they were gonna get from Daddy, but he didn't whip them at all. After he found out my sister was all right, he just gave them boys a good scolding and let them go. I suppose Daddy felt that anybody that crazy had their brains in their butts, and he didn't want to beat what little brains they did have out of them. I don't have to tell you that this ended their less than brilliant career in aviation.

FLYING IN THE FACE OF LIFE

1. Bob + Bob + Bobbit = Lorena (Note: My 'lil brother Bob, the 2nd Bob is what you do when you cut something –when you "bob" something, you are cutting. Bobbit, the last name of the lady accused of cutting.....well, you know what I mean.

2. Before flatware was invented, man always ate with his hands.

3. Most people haven't gone "From the outhouse to the White House"; they had trouble just getting from the outhouse to the church house.

4. If you must look dumb, don't look it by yourself, split it with an equal.

5. Most people will eat anything, as long as you don't tell them what it really is.

6. If man was meant to fly............yeah, yeah, yeah, heard it all before, but the real question is, have you ever heard tell of a two hundred pound bird? (Ostrich not included.)

139

CHAPTER 24

A daddy is as a daddy does

My Daddy was some kind of man --let me tell you! Most people chose to call him Carson and for some reason, that stuck. To tell you the truth, I don't even think he knew his name was Johnny Carcy until he was a grown man. My Mama even named my brother Bob Carson, Junior. I think people would just write down words just like they heard. A good example: It's been told that Grandma Sudie's mama was having a friend of hers "*take down*" a letter for her one time because she could not read nor write. When Great Grandma came to the end of the letter, she ended with Sincerely, (and her name). The friend taking down the letter asked, "How do you spell that Miss Sudie?"

Great Grandma said, "Don't spell it honey, just *write it down*." (Get it?) 'Cause she did not want her to know that she could not spell the name.

As far back as I can remember, Daddy and my brothers use to do quartet gospel singing. Daddy sang bass. It was so funny to see him doing those bass sounds with his mouth. They use to rehearse at our house sometimes and it was so good listening to them. It was my Daddy, my three brothers and a guitar player or two. They could really sing! My brother Bob sounded just like Sam Cooke when he led a song.

They would have a singing engagement just about every Sunday evening at a church somewhere, and the whole family would go to hear them if there was enough transportation for everybody. Yes, times change, but people are basically the same in all of the changing times. The girls use to just hang around my brothers and almost fight over them, right there on the church grounds. I felt kind of special being their little sister, 'cause the girls would "friendly" up to me so they could get close to my brothers. I use to be the message carrier between the boys and those "fast behind" girls. (At least that's what Mama called them.)

My brother Jay Bird was way older than me, so I didn't get to hang or be around him much until I got to be a teenager. I do remember though, that he was a singing human being. He could sing and it would make chill bumps come all over you. He was kind of crazy too. I don't know what it was about singing in public that made people in my family forget what they were supposed to sing. The group used to sing a song called, "I'm Gonna Lay Down my Burdens". One of the boys would lead the verses and sometimes, when it started sounding real good, he would pass the mike to one of the other boys for him to sing the next verse, and that one would then pass the mike to another boy for him to take part in the lead. After Bob had sung,

"Gonna put on my long white robe, down by the riverside, down by the riverside, down by the riverside, gonna put on my long white robe, down by the riverside, and gonna study war no more", he then passed the mike to Jay Bird and Jay Bird belted out, "I'm gonna put on my long white shoes". Well before he could go any further with the song, the audience broke out and started laughing so hard that the quartet stopped singing and started laughing too. But nobody laughed harder than Jay Bird. We teased him about it for a long time.

My Daddy was a real dad. He worked his hind parts off for his family. That man did not have a lazy bone in his body nowhere. By the time we all got up in the mornings, he had already gotten up and made a fire in the stove and milked the cow --when we had one, that is. A lot of times he would have already eaten and gone to the field. You better know that he expected the same from his boys. He believed in an honest day's work, for an honest day's pay. 'Course, we always thought he took it a little further than necessary. He was the first in the field and the last out, no matter what job he was doing. Mama never had to worry about doing anything on the outside of the house. He made sure he and the boys took care of the yards and the wood pile and stuff like that. They would go in the woods and cut down trees and haul the wood back to the house, then they would cut the wood up; we girls would help them stack them close to the pump shed and on the back porch. We did this year round. I don't ever remember not having plenty of wood stored up.

During cotton picking time, Daddy would pick 300 to 350 pounds of cotton a day, all by himself. He would get out real early in the morning and be in the cotton patch by the time the sun came up. He carried a sack slung on each side and picked two rows at a time. When Mama would pick with him, the two of them would pick over 500 pounds. He would put me and my knee baby sister on a row next to his and he would get us started by picking our rows a little ahead of his. Then he would tell us we'd better pick smart so he couldn't catch up with us. He said that if he caught up with us, he was gonna switch us good. He always said that and he always caught up with us, but he never did switch us. I never could figure out how he could pick so much cotton. He took a break when everybody else did and went to dinner when everybody else did, and still he would out pick everybody else in the cotton patch. No, he did not put brickbats, trash, drink bottles, stalks and debris in the sheet like some of the city folks did to make theirs weigh more. No, my Daddy was not deceitful or slick like that. He was an honest man and he was rewarded for that with ability. During these times, the pay was only something like three dollars for every hundred pounds of cotton that you picked. Sad to say, but I never earned three dollars in my whole cotton picking career.

My Daddy could work a mule too. He didn't have to yell and holler at the mule to get her to do what he wanted. Just a few "gee, and haws" and clicking sounds from his lips was all it took. He could plow the prettiest, straightest rows you ever did see. Sometimes I can close my eyes and see my Daddy and that ole mule steady plodding down them long dusty rows in the hot, hot sun, and it makes me so mad. But just like his sweet sister, he never murmured or complained. When I look back on it, I see how he was able to keep on keeping on through it all. It's because he took his responsibilities as a husband and father very seriously. He was proud that he could care for his own. Yes! I am bragging, why not!

I said my Daddy was a good man; I didn't say he wasn't human. He liked to drink a little wine and home brew now and again. There was a big Persimmon Tree across the road from our house, and we young'uns use to eat them like crazy. Did you know if you eat them before they are ripe, they will turn your lips "wrong-si-di-tus", (wrong side out)? Well, they will, and that's a sight to behold. Daddy loved persimmon wine, and he decided to make him some one day. Whatever he had to do to get it started he did it, and he would put it under the house to "work off" –so it can age. Sure enough them pesky brothers of mine took it upon themselves and went under there and drunk the "mash" before it was ready. Please tell me why them boys had no sense. You

144

talking 'bout sick; them boys were sick as pure dogs. When Daddy came home that evening they were lying down with their heads hung off the side of the porch, puking their guts out. He knew right off what the problem was. He said, "You boys been in my stuff, ain't you?" They were so sick they could only moan. So he told them that he was not going to whip them, but that he was just going to let them be as sick as they could get, and that he was not going to let anybody give them any medicine to make them feel better. Also, they had better be up the next morning before he was and ready to go to work. I bet you they thought twice before they stole anymore of Daddy's wine.

Grandpa Travis, my Daddy's dad, lived in Bessemer City, for as long as I can remember. In the Summer, we would go up to visit him and his wife number two, and later, wife number three. Grandpa Travis ran a little store out of his house, and boy, that just suited me. He would give us young'uns all the candy, cookies and Nehi grape sodas we wanted. His third wife was kind of stuck up and didn't care too much for none of us, but Daddy and Mama acted just like they thought the world of her. When we would go on trips and things like that, my favorite place to ride was in the back window of our car. You would get awful tired sitting on somebody's lap for hours and they would get awfully tired of you sitting there too. So after a few miles, I would crawl up in the back window and go to sleep. But they would have to wake me when we rode through downtown Charlotte. That was so exciting! The tall buildings and the traffic just captivated me.

To tell you the truth, I can never recall a time when we didn't have a car. And it was not raggedy and beat up either. The boys made sure that car was always washed and shiny. My Mama didn't drive and never tried to learn either, although out in the country a lot of people drove that didn't have a license.

To me, my Daddy was all that and a bag of chips. He was not scared of anything or anybody, so I thought. Oh, but he was! Bats! A bat could turn that human working machine into a raving lunatic. I know, I saw it happen before. One night a bat flew into the house when one of the boys opened the screen door. Sure enough, Daddy forgot about protecting his wife, his young'uns and anyone else in the room. He caught sight of that bat and took off running through the house, hollering to the tip top of his voice, "Lord knows, there's a bat in here." He made right for the bedroom, ran in, slammed the door and hopped right square in the middle of the bed. He was yelling and jumping straight up and down. We young'uns were running and yelling too, but Mama and Grandma were so tickled at Daddy that they couldn't do nothing but double over laughing. Finally, Brown, my brother-in-law, chased the bat out of the house with a broom. When Daddy came out, he looked like you could have bought him for a penny.

Daddy never called me anything but Goosey and I'm glad. It was sort of something special between us two. He use to sit in the chair and I would get the comb and play in his hair. It wasn't long before he would throw his head back and go fast to sleep, with his mouth wide open. When he went to sleep, especially if he had a little brew in him, he was the hardest person to wake up. We young'uns would gather around his chair and put stuff in his mouth like broom straws or peanuts, and he'd never even stir. Could snore! That man could snore so loud that you could hear it outdoors. He's the only person who I ever heard snore that had a whistle sound along with it. Sometimes it sounded like he was beating a drum and other times it sounded like he fizzled. Whatever sounds he made, believe you me, it could tickle the pure pee out of you.

I hate to say it, but they just don't make men like my Daddy anymore, and that's so sad. We never had to second guess who the head of our household was. Not because he demanded, but because he performed. Not because he was a dominator, but because he was an overseer. Not because he wanted the power, but because he had the strength. Not because he lorded over you, but because he was submissive to the Lord.

DADDIES IN THE KEY OF LIFE

1. A man stands on his name, whatever that might be, while "daddy" holds up the family.

2. "Oh I wished I was in the land of cotton", (You got to be kidding!)

3. Gee, it ain't what you say, but "haw" you say it.

4. It's not the big fierce things that strong men fear, but the little things that show their vulnerability.

5. Watch out Shakespeare, Carcy said it best, "To sleep, per chance to snore."

6. Knowing the HEAD OF ALL THINGS, keeps the rest of the body in order.

CHAPTER 25

<u>Mama, why do we have to move?</u>

God bless the child that has his own. I've always heard that saying and even heard it sung in a song when I was a young'un. But it never really rang true to me until I was about twelve years old.

It seems to me that Winter, when I was a young'un, were much colder and more severe than they are now. It snowed deeper and stayed longer. Just being outdoors for a few minutes made your fingers and toes feel like they were stuck together. The chimney was always billowing with thick smoke and the windows of the house were always frosted. Icicles hung from the corners of the roofs just beckoning us young'uns to break them off and suck them. 'Course Mama warned us that doing this would make us have "The Sore Throat." We didn't care about that and every chance we'd get, we'd suck them to our hearts' content.

It used to snow so high that it would bank up to our porch and create a giant slide affect. We would get toebagging sacks and sit on them and slide off the porch on the frozen snow, down to the ditch. That was the "best" fun you could ever imagine. We'd stay out as long as Mama and the others would let us and then we'd run in the house half frozen and head straight for the heater. Have you ever held your frozen fingers over a warm stove? Well, don't! You talking about pain! It feels like somebody is sticking five hundred million needles in your hands. We were told over and over not to do that and yet again, we did; young'uns ain't got no sense. You're supposed to rub your fingers together to warm them gradually. We would be jumping up and down; they would be hurting so bad. But as soon as they thawed out, we were right back outdoors again.

Living on a farm means that there is not a whole lot of work to be done in the Winter except maybe grading a little dry tobacco. So the winters were sort of lean as far as having cash on hand. We would have some food that was canned and preserved in the Summer, and some cured meat from the Winter before. But we all know that there are things that you just got to have money for. But even to me, this particular Winter seemed extremely hard on us.

My brothers were courting boys by this time and they liked to look nice for the girls. They needed to put gas in the car and pay for stuff when they took their girlfriends out. Daddy and Mama just didn't have the money to give them. So the boys decided that they wanted to go and get a public job working in the tobacco factory so they could have money of their own and help with the household expenses too. There was not much work on the farm to do, so Daddy allowed them to go get a public job.

You would have thought that they had committed murder or something when the owner of the farm found out. He didn't have any work for them to do, yet he didn't want them working anywhere else. He demanded that Daddy make the boys quit their public jobs. Daddy said that he would not do that because he didn't see any reason for it. He told the man that he would keep working on the farm himself even though he needed more work and more money too. But the owner got the devil in him and demanded that we move off his property --that same week, mind you. There were not a lot of empty houses to rent in the country. What do you do when you ain't got no money but you have to find someplace to go in the spare of the moment? You do whatever you can do and you depend on the Lord and trust Him with the rest.

I couldn't believe that this man was treating us this way. This was the same man that came to our house one Christmas Eve and brought two big beautifully wrapped packages for me and my knee baby sister. We were so excited, I thought we were going to take wings and fly. He insisted that we open our present while he watched. I was overcome with happiness and sheer excitement. We grabbed those boxes and would have ripped them open in a milli-second if my Mama had not made us slow down so we could save the pretty wrapping paper and ribbon. In my mind's eye, I imagined a beautiful bridal doll, or a tea set with china plates, and even a sparkly pair of plastic high heels with the sparkly pocketbook to match. By the time we got to the tissue wrapping, we were both giddy with anticipation. When we pulled back the last piece of tissue on our gift, there lying ever so boldly was ONE lonely Tootsie Roll Pop. My heart sank, and my voice went right out the window. I could not speak. I stood transfixed; in fact, I was mesmerized while staring at that box with eyes the size of a fifty cent piece. Suddenly, my brothers and some of the others burst out laughing, which made me and my sister began an abundance of great wailing sobs. I looked at Mama and I could tell that she did not think it was funny, not one bit; and when I looked at the man, he was laughing so hard, tears were rolling down his face. I thought he would never stop, but finally he did. Then he walked back to his pickup truck and turned to me and Sudie Mae and said, "Early in the morning come and knock at the back door and say, Christmas gift and see what happens." That's all he said and he drove away. Mama scolded the boys --all of them for laughing at us and began to share her thoughts and opinion of why someone who would play such a cruel trick on innocent little young'uns. She even said that if she was us, that she would not go up to the house on Christmas morning. She said she wished we could afford to buy him a really nice present to make him feel ashamed of himself.

Bright and early the next morning after we had gotten up to see what Santa Claus had brought us, I decided that I was going up to the "big house" and say what he told me to say. So off I go, not knowing what to expect this time. Sure enough, as soon as I knocked at the door, he appeared and I said, "Christmas gift". He handed me a not so big package this time, but it was just as beautifully wrapped as the others had been the day before. I was itching to open it but was scared to. So I ran home with it as fast as I could. When I got home I went straight to where Mama was and tore the wrapping off. Lo and behold, she was the prettiest little doll that I ever did see, with long brown hair that hung almost to her feet and she was the height from my wrist to my elbow. I stuck out my chest and my tongue and paraded her around to all the people that had laughed so hard at me before. I suppose Sudie Mae got her present later, 'cause she didn't go with me that morning.

Now, back to the move. How could the same tender hearted person turn so cold? I don't know. Maybe in a way he felt that he owned us body and soul. Daddy had to sell what hogs we had cause there was no place to keep them. I guess this was good in a way, in that it put a little money in Daddy's pocket. Daddy seemed real quiet and kind of sad that week. I heard Mama keep telling him not to worry, that the Lord would make a way somehow. It wasn't like we hoped, but by the end of the week, He had.

Daddy found a house for us to move into about a mile from where we were living. It was this big monster of a house that was covered in red tar paper. It sat way back off the road between two sweet potato fields. There was no spicket (faucet) in the kitchen like we had at our other house, but there was a well on the back porch. The house had only four rooms but they were big enough to put two beds apiece in each one. The house was almost falling down. You could look around the edges of the floors and see the ground underneath the house, and you could actually see the sky through the ceilings. There was a fireplace in the middle room and a place in the front room where you could put a wood stove. I hated it!

It was the coldest house I had ever been in –in my life. No matter how much wood you put on the fire, you never got warm unless you were in the middle room or unless you were about four feet from the fire itself. You could feel the cold air coming up from beneath the house. If you left water in a glass or bucket in any room other than the middle room, the water would be a solid cake of ice within a few hours, especially at night. We had to sleep with a toboggin on our heads 'cause the cold air would blow down from the cracks in the ceiling. We slept under layers of quilts and blankets and even piled clothes on the bed in real frigid weather. I remember Mama having one of them old smoothing irons, and she would put it in the fireplace and let it get real hot. Then she wrapped it in some old rags and put it under the covers at the foot of the bed to keep our feet warm. Hey, we had to do what we had to do! We didn't have any money, so we did the best we could with what we had. Mama always said that the Lord would bless our efforts. It appeared to me He did, for none of us ever froze.

I don't know about you, but there are some memories that I will carry with me to my grave or during "that great getting up morning" or when Jesus returns in the "twinkling of an eye". On one of the coldest mornings that I can remember in my whole life, I was walking down the path to catch the school bus when I looked over in the sweet potato field to my left. There, I saw my Daddy and Mama with hoes, trying to break through the frozen earth to get to the sweet potatoes left there by the diggers. Just to get enough to feed us another meal or two. They looked up and saw me and waved, and the pain and humiliation in their eyes could not be hidden. I wanted to scream to the top of my lungs, but I just ran all the rest of the way to the highway, with tears streaming down my face. Even today, when I am reminded of that scene in my mind, I feel sad and I hurt on the inside. My Daddy was broken and his pride was crushed all because of someone's hateful heart and selfishness.

We scrapped cotton, (picked after the cotton picker had gone through the fields), sheeted tobacco for whomever we could, and found whatever odd jobs we could do to see us through that Winter.

On Saturday, I helped an old man and his wife after school around their house. I hung out clothes, swept and dusted the house and carried in wood and stuff like that. On the Saturdays I worked there, the wife would let me eat lunch with them (the same time, but not in the same location) but she fed me on the back porch. You know, I didn't even know that I was supposed to be offended by this, so I wasn't. It was just another day in the neighborhood.

Up until this time, I could not recall Mama ever being sick. But she got a terrible case of the flu while we lived in this house, and was bedridden for a long spell. Then Daddy got the flu before she got well and they both were down at the same time. I did the best I could and my sisters came and helped as much as possible. It really scared me to see them both so sick like this so I stayed home from school to look after them. I was young, but having to help take care of Grandma Sudie had prepared me for looking after sick folks. Thank the good Lord, finally, they both recovered and no one else in the house came down with it. Daddy said they got sick because that old big barn of a house was too drafty.

The well was on the back porch and in the mornings, sometimes when the temperature was below freezing, we would have to take something and break through the solid sheet of ice on the surface of the water before we could draw a bucket. This would make you not even care about washing your face, much less other parts. Then you'd have to put the water on the stove to heat it enough to wash in. Some mornings there would be grits or oatmeal for breakfast and other mornings we would eat what was left from supper. It might be pinto beans and corn bread, backbones and rice (you know, like neckbones) or sweet potatoes and field peas and biscuits. Whatever it was, I was glad to get it and never even thought about complaining, 'cause I knew how hard it had been to come by. Maybe young'uns these days need to know that and they might not be so picky.

Don't get me wrong. All the times spent in that house were not terrible. We still had Saturday nights around the television and Sundays when the whole family would come together. One Saturday night Mama and Daddy had driven into town to visit my sister Lois. My brother Bob and I were the only ones home. We got hungry and decided we would fix us some French fries. So we cut up about four big potatoes and got about three pounds of lard hot in a big cast iron skillet (not hot enough, mind you, but we didn't know). We fried them potatoes, but they came out limp and dripping with grease. We devoured them anyway. Honey chile hush! In just a little while, our stomachs sounded like somebody was moving furniture around in them. Lordy, I broke out in sweat and just did make it to the edge of the yard before my belly erupted. I looked behind me and here comes Bob running, his belly doing the same thing. Five minutes later I was sprinting for the outhouse and Bob was darting for the corn field. This went on most of the night. We two crazy young'uns were sick as hound dogs. When we burped, it cleared out the house. Mama said that we had a case of the "sour belly", from cooking them fries in too much grease that was *not* hot enough. All I know is that the sour belly is not something I want to have ever again.

We made it through though, in spite of the house and the circumstances. Daddy and Mama even managed to save a few pennies for a down payment on a small house in Dunn.

Thank you Lord, thank you! We be moving to town!!!

LIFE PASSAGES

1. Hard times make for heavy hearts, but hearty determinations.

2. Things you own, places you own, but people you can never own. The price for them has already been paid.

3. It's not about where you live or what you live in, but how you live in it.

4. A sour belly or a sour disposition; both of them can run folks away.

5. When you think you can't, you can. When you don't want to, you will. When you have to, nothing can stop you.

6. Don't worry so much about breaking the ice, sometimes you have to, to get to the water.

EPILOGUE

Inside all of us are stories from our days as young'uns that bring back all kinds of feelings and sad memories; some are good and some not so good. But these are the experiences that can (if we allow them), shape our lives positively and/or negatively. It's not the circumstances in our past that make us the folks that we are, but the way we relate to them and the attitudes with which we live beyond them.

We were created with the capacity to love, to laugh, to enjoy and, yes, even to overcome. As the old saying goes, "Tain't nuttin to it, but to do it." So what if you were born on the wrong side of the track. (*Who* determines which side is right and which side is wrong anyway.) Just come to the realization that the side of the track you did come from was where you were meant to blossom and excel; in other words, allow some good to come out of your life no matter which side. So what if you came from plain poor folks. Just take those good morals and values, and the simple pleasures you experienced in your life and allow them the many opportunities to keep you grounded and humble. So what if others looked down on you. Use that as a lesson to never look down on someone else. So, what about race and prejudice --and all that? What about em! Hey, everybody you meet is not going to love you – and it won't always be because of your skin color either. You just be the best person you can be and do the best at all things that you can; now, how folks feel about you – well let that be their hang up and not yours.

All I know is that we are here to bring glory to GOD who wonderfully and fearfully made us in the likeness and image of HIMSELF. We are not here to bemoan and groan about the life we were given, but to embrace it and share it with others.

I hope, that by sharing some of my life with you, it has brought you a little joy and maybe even brought alive some good memories that lie just beneath the surface of your heart.

Be blessed, until we meet again on the pages of Life in Town.

AUTHOR'S BIO

Age 9

I was born November 22 in the year nineteen hundred and fifty. My Daddy and Mama were Jimmy and Luretha; two young people who started dating in high school and took on the responsibilities of parenthood way too early.

My mother died from complications of childbirth when I was only 3 months old, and my Daddy thought it best to leave me with my maternal grandparents, Carcy, always called Carson and Mary Florence. From that day forward, I became their child. No formal adoption was necessary. Back then, people took care of their own, without question or pause. I'm so glad they did! John, Thomas, Carson Junior, Lois, Shirley and Sudie Mae became my brothers and sisters and that was just the way it was. I attended elementary schools in Johnston County and high school in Harnett County. The County integrated schools in 1968; I completed my senior year at the white school in my hometown. I also accomplished a milestone by being the only child in my family to graduate.

I married my dear sweetheart, Ordie; of course, afterwards we started our family, our delightful children -- Roderick, Erica and Tracey. I've worked in factories and cotton mills; I've worked as a maid and a nanny; I've worked as an office clerk and served as a food services director. For the last sixteen years I have

managed the North Carolina Supreme Court Printing
Department. My greatest achievement was over forty
years ago, when I made Jesus Christ the Lord of my
life. Everything I have and everything I am --or ever
will be --is because of Him!

CPSIA information can be obtained
at www.ICGtesting.com
Printed in the USA
LVOW12s1451070218
565637LV00002B/93/P